I HAVE TWO WORDS FOR YOU

*A Story of One Woman's Journey to
Healing, Freedom, and Faith*

JAMIE DAHL

EMPOWERYOU
PUBLISHING

I Have Two Words For You
Published by EMpowerYOU Publishing

For booking information visit: https://thedahliadiaries.com/contact

Cover designed by EMpowerYOU Publishing
Cover photos by Whitney Wiatt

First U.S. Edition: May 2019

ISBN: 978-1-7327916-2-6

Table of Contents

Introduction

For years I have believed that all things work together for good and that positive outcomes are possible even when life hurls a major curveball in your direction. Those curveballs can come in all forms and some, in my opinion, look like a big, fat, rotten tomato in the kisser. But in reality, I never had to truly experience the truth of that statement until I got the call that no woman wants to receive. That call with a voice on the other end that says, "You have breast cancer." In an instant, my life was changed forever.

Now, this is the crazy part. I'm a young, healthy woman with no genetic marker or history of the disease yet at the age of forty-three I was being told that I was going to have to get in the boxing ring, pull up my big girl pants, and fight for my life. All I could think of at that moment was, "I seriously don't have time for this! I have a family, a career, and a social life! I can't possibly put my world on hold to deal with this mess!" But that is exactly what I had to do. Up until this point, I was clicking along living the American dream. I was married to Andrew, the love of my life (still am), and raising two young daughters, Lauren and Katherine, ages six and seven and a half. I had a diverse and exciting career resume, was actively participating as a community volunteer, and had two casseroles in the freezer ready to heat up at any moment. How could a nightmare like this happen to me? Well, it did, and this book is about that rollercoaster journey. But before I take you down that road, I think it's important to tell you a little bit more about how I tick.

There are a few ingredients that when mixed together pretty much sum me up. If you combine a scoop of kindness, a pinch of spunk, some tenacity, a spoonful of wit, along with the fear of not being perfect, and despite my previous dance career, a healthy helping of clumsiness, that's me. However, the most essential part of what makes up Jamie Dahl is my faith in God. From a very young age, my parents instilled in me a strong belief in Jesus and the importance of having a personal relationship with Him. Granted, it has taken years for me to develop that relationship, and I believe everyone's faith journey is different. I have grown from praying for a passing grade on my middle school math test to earnestly seeking God's will, His plan, and His purpose in my life. Even with all of that progress, I am still growing, learning, and making a lot of mistakes along the way. As I look back on each chapter of my breast cancer story, I see that God, not me, is the main character. Even though you will hear my voice, hopefully you will relate to me as a fellow woman, and travel alongside me over the peaks and valleys of my emotional landscape. God is indeed the hero in these pages. And honestly, I didn't know how big of a part He would play until the rubber hit the road and my world fell apart.

As I navigated through my diagnosis and treatment, I found comfort in writing. It wasn't often, but when I felt impressed to journal what I was feeling or learning, I grabbed my trusty iPad and off to the porch I went. It became therapeutic to remove the swirling thoughts and emotions in my brain by channeling them through my fingers and onto the screen. It helped me to sort out my questions, to reflect on consistent themes I was noticing in my life, and to give myself a place to be real and vulnerable. I chose to post these thoughts on my Facebook page and was overwhelmed by the response I received. Not only did I feel incredibly supported and encouraged, but I found that there were a lot of people who were going through difficulties, too. People who were looking for someone who could relate to their pain, their fears, and their struggles. So, I made a conscious decision to allow myself to be transparent and to let them see my pain, my fears, and my struggles with the desire that it may give them hope and comfort.

Everyone is at a different place in their lives, and everyone's story is different. Some people are struggling with divorce, death, physical or mental abuse, or disease, just to name a few. Unfortunately, there is so much pain in this world, and I believe that pain is pain. It comes in many different forms, and we will all experience some type of it at some point in our lives. How we approach these moments is unique for everyone.

For me, I am a believer in Jesus Christ, and He is my rock who I run to in both calm waters and when my ship is going down. This may be the same for you. You may share these same beliefs and lean heavily on the principles of the Bible and are looking for examples of other Christian women and how they relied on their faith for comfort. Or, maybe you grew up in a Christian home, but all that really meant to you was an annoying early wakeup call every Sunday when you were forced to go to church with the family. You may be curious as to how this whole "God" thing works and how it can actually be applied to your life in a real way and more than just church on Sunday. Or, you may be someone who doesn't believe in God at all. Having a personal relationship with Jesus might sound really hokey and corny to you. Trusting in a God that right now you can only experience in fluffy paintings with cherubs sitting on clouds doesn't feel real to you one bit. Maybe in your mind, the thought of believing and trusting in a higher power signifies that you are weak in some way and that you can't handle your life on your own. But, regardless of where you're at, you're hurting, and you need some answers. I get that.

No matter where you fall on that spectrum regarding your beliefs, I encourage you to keep reading. My most significant pain moment came for me through my breast cancer diagnosis. I genuinely believe that there are lessons that I learned through this difficult time that will apply to you no matter where you are in your journey or what your story may be. An open heart and a teachable spirit are all that is needed to hopefully gather a few good nuggets that might help you navigate through this crazy and unpredictable life.

Through this trial, I learned that we have a choice. We can choose to react to the junk that life throws at us like my daughters did when they were toddlers by kicking and screaming, whining, pounding their fists into the rug, and throwing a pity party because life wasn't being fair. Or, we can choose to have the attitude that this experience can grow us and strengthen our resolve. Now, don't get me wrong. I had those kicking and screaming moments, but I chose not to live there. I decided that I was going to allow God to use it for His glory and His divine purposes, and I realized that maybe my life isn't supposed to be just about....me. I chose to find the beauty that can come from the ugly and the learning that can come from the lessons.

One of my goals of this book is to help you see that there is hope no matter your situation. My prayer is that my story will help show you how to trust God from the valley that you may be hunkered down in, while you are waiting to see the sun come up over the mountain top. The most important thing that I hope takes a firm hold of your heart when you have read the last page and close this book is that God will never leave you nor forsake you. As Fancy Nancy, my daughter's beloved literary character would say, "forsake" is just a fancy word for leave. Think abandon, cast aside, or discard. Nope. God's not going to do any of those things. Even during those times when you think there is entirely no hope, you are at the end of your rope, or you are literally looking death in the face, He will not leave you. In fact, in those moments if you press that much harder into Him and surrender your desire to be in control, He will show His incredible love for you in ways you never imagined. I'm walking proof of that. My hope is by inviting you into my world and letting you see the good, the bad, and the ugly, you will get a glimpse of how God demonstrates His fierce love for us.

My guess is that you have this book in your hands for a reason. Your world may have just stopped on a dime as mine did, and you're looking for hope and answers. If I had one wish, it would be to have the ability to jump through these pages and sit next to you with a hot cup of coffee, a box of tissues, and endless amounts of time. I would hold back the temptation to tell you, "This is going to be easy. It's only a blip on your radar". Instead, I would be honest with you, be real and help you understand that this is going to be a battle. But, through this fight, you will uncover things about yourself you never knew.

During that time together, I would provide a safe space for you to comfortably express what you are truly feeling. An environment where you can put all of the emotions that we so often hide when we are hurting, on the table. It's those emotions and responses people don't really want to see or hear when they genuinely ask, "How are you?" And, I would let you ask the questions that are heavy on your heart about your family, losing your hair, or even your relationship with your spouse or significant other. Those things you feel you can't discuss with your neighbor, or even a close family member because it just feels too personal, or they couldn't possibly understand.

Here's how this is going to work. In Part One, I'm going to let you come alongside me as I share my story with breast cancer. This is my raw, honest truth about what it is like to walk through this trial. As you immerse yourself into my world, you will experience the peaks and valleys that I encountered, and be able to see it all through my eyes.

In Part Two, I will share some of the most important lessons I have learned. Both the revelations that God revealed in my heart and the practical survival tips I wish someone had shared with me. You may find things that you will need to authentically process in your own heart. I would hope the space within these pages is a safe harbor for you to do just that. Hold my hand and let's travel this road together.

Get ready to hop on the rollercoaster I call my "cancer journey." Grab a cup of coffee or your favorite organic, loose leaf, citrus and ginkgo green tea, and get comfy. But, buckle up because you're about to jump on my crazy train! Here we go!

PART ONE

1

Baby Proof

*"Now faith is confidence in what we hope for and assurance about
what we do not see."*
Hebrews 11:1

The sun was sparkling off the waves of the Mississippi River as I dug my little eight-year-old toes into the warm sand of the riverside beach. I was spending this beautiful summer day with my mom playing in the water, building sand castles and just being a kid. She had a blanket spread out for us, and I'm sure a healthy snack or two. The time leisurely sauntered by as all good summer days do when you're a child. Little did I know that God was going to use this moment to teach me a vital lesson about the power of prayer and demonstrate what it feels like to have childlike faith.

After a full morning of sun, it was time for us to pack up the shovels and buckets and head back to the car. As I was walking barefoot through the sand to the parking lot, I inadvertently stepped on a sandbur bush. If you're not familiar with sandburs, I believe this particular flora was made by the devil. Well, not really, but dog-gone it, they are nasty little buggers!

A sandbur is a weed that grows in sandy soils and during the summer months produces spiny burs about the size of a pea. These burs look like a mini version of a medieval ball flail weapon you would see a knight hurl at his opponent, but with added hooks on the end of the spikes. Imagine stepping on a whole stem of these with soft little feet. The pain I felt shoot through my foot was intense.

I began to cry and my mom scooped me up in her arms and carried me to the car. She sat me down on the front seat and gingerly pried the burs out of my skin. Even after they had been removed, the stinging sensation remained. It felt as though my foot was on fire and I wanted nothing more than for that feeling to go away, but I could tell that wasn't going to happen anytime soon.

We pulled out of the parking lot and headed for home. As we curved down the winding road, my mom began to explain to me that we can pray to God to heal our hurts, and because she was my mom and kids that age pretty much believe everything their parents tell them, I trusted her. I wasn't really sure how it all worked, but I listened and tried to blink back my tears as she started to explain that all I had to do was ask God to take the pain away. Holding my aching foot in my hand, I closed my eyes and quietly whispered in my mind, "Jesus, please make my foot feel better." It was simple. It was short. I didn't go on and on about how healing my foot would change my life, and how I would use this experience to start a ministry to rid the world of sandburs. I didn't bargain and plead my case about how I would never walk barefoot again or list all the reasons why I thought He should heal me. No. I simply asked, and trusted. I trusted with child-like faith because that's all I knew. My need was immediate, and I didn't know where else to turn. I really didn't know if He would relieve my pain, but I gave it a shot because I was suffering.

What happened next has been seared in my mind since that sunny summer day all those years ago. The instant that I finished uttering those few simple words in my head the pain was gone. Now please understand, this wasn't just a little ache that may have felt like it lessened a little. No, this was a searing, burning feeling that was immediately relieved. I absolutely could not believe what had just happened, and yet it didn't really shock me because my mommy had told me that I could ask God to help me and mommies are always right! So, one part of my eight-year-old mind thought, "Did that really happen? My pain is completely gone! This doesn't make sense!" And the other part of my mind was thinking, "Well, of course, it happened. That's what God does. He hears and answers our prayers."

I believe that I was given this opportunity as a child so that I would physically experience the healing power of God and recognize His intense love for me. Have I spoken many prayers since then that haven't been answered as immediately and as precisely as this one? Absolutely. But I trust that God is still hearing each and every one of my prayers and answers them in a way that only a good father does. When I experienced this miraculous moment as a child, it set the stage for my faith walk. The foundation was beginning to be built one stone at a time in order for me to have the courage to get through a battle my tender eight-year-old self would never have thought was in store for me. God used those sandburs, a tiny bit of faith, and the act of trust, to give me proof that He was real.

2

Sugar Insanity

"Yet I am always with you; you hold me by my right hand."
Psalm 73:23-24

The back of my car was packed with multi-colored presents adorned with fluffy bows, boxes of decorations, a cake, and two giddy little girls excited about what most little girls get crazy excited about -- a birthday party! My youngest daughter, Katherine, was turning seven and loved anything that had to do with the theater. She was born accepting her Oscar award and has been practicing her dramatic skills since the first time she opened her eyes. She is always singing, pretending, making up stories and characters, and so it only seemed appropriate for her sixth birthday party to have an acting theme.

Okay, moms, what is it about the themes? Kids are all about themes, and many of you are Pinterest masterminds that create these dreamy wonderlands of lollipops and rainbows, and I am seriously in awe of you. You are able to effortlessly match the ribbons on the chair covers to the homemade life-size piñata of Barbie you whipped up the night before. I think that's amazing! Lately, I typically find myself struggling to get text message invites out on the fly and praying that I'm still in the Amazon Prime window for free two-day shipping for birthday presents.

However, I had managed to get in a little pre-planning this time around and begged a children's acting teacher at our local community theater to do an acting class party for us. When we arrived, my mother and father and I frantically ran around one of the classrooms decking it out with a little red carpet, some gold stars that we stuck on the walls with painters' tape, and a box of old costumes I brought from home. After the appropriate sprucing up was completed, we plopped down in a couple of chairs lined against the wall and did some deep breathing exercises as we mentally prepared ourselves for the onslaught of six-year-old wanna-be movie stars.

They poured in armed with gift bags and frenzied excitement. It was officially "go time." We jumped into action, corralling the adorable little rascals and taking pictures like a pack of paparazzi. The acting teacher was brilliant as she molded and directed and redirected them into a relatively organized troupe that gave an adorable performance they helped to create. We all clapped and cheered and then I said the magic words. "Time for cake!" You'd think they had been told that this was the last taste of sugar they would ever experience in their lifetimes. They sprinted for the table, decorated with some pretty pathetic Comedy and Tragedy masks that I whipped up after a panicked trip to Hobby Lobby, and descended upon the dessert. We all sang a sweetly off-tune rendition of "Happy Birthday", and the table full of little girls quickly devoured multiple plates of cake and ice cream.

The party was a hit, and each child left happy and appropriately sugar-buzzed. We broke down the decorations, loaded the gifts in the car, and then stuck around to scrub the tape off the floor from the fake red carpet we used with the "easily removable" built-in adhesive. At least that's what the package said. Oh sure. Thankfully, one of the moms stayed to help me painstakingly pick the pieces of tape off of the previously impeccable floor. See, that's what friends do. They make sure you're not alone while you internally curse the company that makes so called removable fake red carpets, the guy that created the tape, and the lady who sold you the carpet at the party store.

Once we finished that formidable task, I took my raw fingertips and two exhausted daughters and headed home with my husband. Check. That was done. One more birthday party in the books and onto the next thing on my ever-growing, never-ending to-do list that was my life. I was a busy mom that was always on the move. I had errands to run, a business to manage, two children to care for, and many other important things that kept me in the constant hustle. I was like many other women and mothers out there getting up day in and day out, taking inventory of what had been accomplished, and what still needed to be conquered. I didn't have time for distractions or obstacles. I had things to do! But little did I know, an obstacle was right around the corner. Actually, I don't even think you could call it that. An obstacle is something you need a little effort to get around, but then you keep right on going. No, this was more like a massive, scary, stop-you-in-your-tracks and knock-you-to-the-ground barricade.

3

Wait, What?

"The Lord is good, a stronghold in the day of trouble; he knows those who take refuge in him."
Nahum 1:7

Two days after my daughter's birthday party, I was feeling slightly recovered and attacking Monday morning like any other. Kids up and dressed, check. Lunches packed, check. Teeth relatively brushed, check. I piled the girls into the car and off we went to school. After they were safely inside, I was sitting in my car in the parking lot checking some emails and mapping out my plan of attack for the day. I heard a tap on my window, and when I looked up, I saw another mom, and friend, who had just dropped her children off at school that morning as well. She and I had known each other for years, were both enjoying this season of watching our children grow up together and were both in full "mom mode."

I rolled down my window, and as she leaned her arm on my car, I noticed she had a strange look on her face. She took a breath and said, "I have breast cancer." The first word out of my mouth was, "What?" I was absolutely shocked, and my mind started spinning with all of the "how's." How was this even possible? How does this happen to someone who's so young and healthy? How does cancer affect someone so close to me? Up until this point, cancer had not reared its ugly head within my peer group, and the fact that this was happening to her was blowing my mind. My family had unfortunately lost loved ones to this disease, but most of them had long life journeys. Losing a loved one, no matter what age, is difficult but when a disease like this begins to affect those within your own age group, it's incredibly sobering. Hearing her say those few explosive words was a massive reality check.

For about fifteen minutes, she shared with me a few more details of her diagnosis. As we were talking, I got this strange, sinking feeling inside. About a month and a half prior, I remember feeling a small lump about the size of a pea in my right breast. Honestly, I don't even remember how I felt the lump. It may have been when I was getting dressed one morning, but the exact moment escaped me. I remembered telling my husband about it while standing in the kitchen one evening, but even then, my reaction was pretty nonchalant and resembled something like, "Huh, this is weird. Check this out." Neither of us really thought too much about it at the time. It didn't hurt, and it wasn't terribly close to the skin, but I could feel it. I shrugged it off as fibrous tissue, or possibly a fluid-filled cyst, and even googled "breast tissue changes during menstrual cycles" thinking it had something to do with that. Needless to say, at that time I wasn't rushing to get it checked by my physician. Just three and a half months earlier I had a routine mammogram, and everything was fine. So, the red flags weren't waving very loudly for me and, I think like many women, I was busy taking care of everyone else and had put my needs high on the shelf to take down later and address only when the time was more convenient.

Toward the end of my conversation with my friend there in the school parking lot, I shared with her that I had found a lump. I told her that because of everything she had just shared with me, I was going to go home immediately to make an appointment to have it looked at. I called my primary care physician. I remember the hint of concern in her voice and the sense of urgency in which she made the appointment for a mammogram two days later. All of a sudden, the unknowns were staring me in the face like headlights on a speeding Mack truck. I could almost feel the blinding glare of those lights and the terrifying anticipation of the collision. However, I fully believed, at that time, that this was routine and that my initial thoughts of the lump being completely harmless would be confirmed. I mean, really? I had just had a clean mammogram only a few months prior. So naturally, I was just fine, right?

4

I Don't Know What This Is

"So do not fear, for I am with you..."
Isaiah 41:10

The day came for my appointment, and I sat in the waiting room of the Center for Breast Care, waiting for my buzzer to go off. I was scheduled for both a mammogram and an ultrasound, just to rule anything serious out. I scrolled through Facebook and answered a few emails, and then jumped slightly when the pager on my lap vibrated and began blinking red. I handed it to the nurse who guided me back to the changing room. She showed me a metal locker to put my belongings in and handed me a soft, white, waffle weave robe to put on.

She led me into the imaging room, and I prepared to get pressed from every side. Looking back now, that was both literally and figuratively! Those of you who have been up close and personal with a mammography machine know what I'm talking about. I am grateful for this machine and what it does, but seriously people, with all of the technology we have these days, you would think someone could design a device that wasn't the twenty-first century version of medieval torture! The squishing and squeezing and holding your breath is enough to send a gal to therapy!

After my breasts had been flattened to resemble lumpy pancakes and all of the appropriate images had been taken, the mammography tech led me into another room to wait for my ultrasound. The nurse was a delightful woman who did a wonderful job of making this experience as tolerable as possible. We chatted a little, and I shared with her that I had two daughters and offered a few other pieces of information that you volunteer during the slightly awkward small talk after a stranger has just seen you naked from the waist up.

I was called back for my ultrasound, and I hopped up on the exam table and waited for the radiologist to come in. There was a desk on one side of the room with a computer, and the ultrasound equipment and monitors were positioned near the head of the table. The radiologist came in, greeted me and explained how the ultrasound was going to take place. The mammography tech dimmed the lights, and I immediately thought how nice this was to take a break from my busy day and rest in this quiet darkened room for a little while. I think that's why I like going to the dentist. I'm forced to lay on a comfy chair with my feet up, uninterrupted for a minimum of 30 minutes. With that same mindset, I was going to make the most of this appointment, close my eyes, and sneak a rare power nap. But as I typically do, I laid there with my daily to-do list ticking through my head like the board on the New York Stock Exchange; go to Target, grab dinner for tonight, send that email I meant to do yesterday, pack a snack for the girls before dance class.

My thoughts bounced back and forth about the rest of the day ahead of me as the ultrasound wand slid around on a layer of gunky messy gel. After about 20 minutes of silence, only interrupted by the quiet whirring and clicking of the machine, I was jolted back to the present by the radiologist's voice saying, "Jamie, I'd like you to take a look at something." I sat up and turned to face the monitor that was hovering over my head. She began to point out a white mass in the middle of my left breast that didn't look like the rest of my other breast tissue. She pointed to it and said the words that have been seared in my mind ever since. "I don't know what this is." She began to explain that she would like to do a biopsy of the spot in question and recommended that I have the procedure done immediately. She gave me the option of waiting and making the appointment at another time but strongly encouraged me to do it right then. My mind began spinning, and for a split second, I didn't know how to answer her. I was wrestling with wanting to talk to my husband first to have his support during the procedure, and yet wanting to get this over with while I was right here. I decided to have the biopsy right then since she was able to fit me in, and honestly, I was a little frightened by her urgency and willingness to shift her schedule to accommodate me.

She left the room to get the instruments and the additional staff that she needed. I sat waiting and alone in the dark while the mammography tech clicked away at the computer keyboard with her back to me. I've never experienced a darkened room go blacker without the help of turning down the lights, but that is precisely what happened. I could feel the heaviness of the darkness begin to envelop me and the reality of what was happening came crashing down. It was as though someone had thrown a bucket of ice water in my face and I realized that this was serious. There was a very good chance that something was terribly wrong with me, and all of a sudden, my "oh so necessary" trip to Target didn't seem so important anymore.

I sat on the end of the table with my heart pounding and the tech, still with her back to me, started cheerfully asking about my daughters. As soon as she mentioned my babies, I burst into tears. My mind started racing with thoughts like, "I have to be here for my girls. I can't die. There's so much I need to teach them yet. What will happen to them if I'm gone?" She heard me catch my breath and my soft sniffles and she spun around in her rolling chair to face me. Still sitting down, she said, "Can I pray with you?" All I could muster was a nod and a soft "Yes." She held my hands and began praying for me. She prayed the most beautiful, encouraging, heartfelt prayer with conviction and power. I can't tell you the exact words because my mind was in such turmoil that I probably couldn't have even told you my name had I been asked, but I do remember feeling a sense of peace wash over me on that cold hospital table.

Just as she was finishing her prayer, the radiologist walked in with two other nurses rolling a table of instruments that looked a little scary and a lot intimidating. They came in with an air of seriousness, and there was an immediate flurry of activity that changed the feel of the room from a relaxing oasis to a somber, procedural environment.

I held my breath while the doctor did the biopsy. I have never felt so alone in my life. No one knew what I was going through at that very moment.

I couldn't even text my husband because my phone was locked in the dressing room locker with all of my clothing. I was living this nightmare entirely by myself and was overcome with a sense of isolation. It was only me, God, and the other professionals in the room that had any idea what was happening to me.

After what seemed like an eternity of poking, prodding, some painful needle sticks, and a lot of weird clicking sounds, the biopsy was finished. The radiologist put a bandage on the small wound, I put my spa robe on and I shuffled back to the dressing room. My head was spinning, and I felt a little woozy, not because of the procedure but because my brain was numb. Numb with fear, numb with shock, and numb with the unknown.

My angel (a.k.a. "The Praying Mammography Tech") came into the dressing room and asked how I was doing. I thanked her profusely for her thoughtfulness, and most importantly, her prayer. I told her that I shared her faith in God and how meaningful and helpful that simple act of kindness had been for me at that horrible moment. She sweetly replied, "This is my ministry."

Never have I ever had a medical professional pray with me in a clinical setting. I firmly believe that God specifically placed her in that exam room at that exact moment. He used her to speak to me in a way that only He knew would be comforting for me. This was His way of beginning to show me that He was never going to leave my side during what was going to be a long, difficult road. Even though I had walked with the Lord most of my life, it was as though He was introducing Himself to me for the first time on a whole different level. He used this faithful woman to very practically demonstrate Isaiah 41:10 which says, *"So do not fear, for I am with you; do not be dismayed, for I am your God. I will strengthen you and help you; I will uphold you with my righteous right hand."* It wasn't until later when I would recognize how profound this truth would be in my life.

5

We Need to Talk

"The name of the Lord is a fortified tower; the righteous run to it and are safe."
Proverbs 18:10

I left the hospital and walked in a complete daze to my car in the parking lot. I don't really remember how I got there, but somehow my feet went into autopilot. I slid into the driver's seat, closed the door, put my hands on the steering wheel and dissolved into a puddle of tears. I cried one of those deep, guttural cries that feel as though your insides are exploding. I didn't know what to do or where to go next. The only thing I knew was that I needed to talk to my husband.

I collected myself and drove straight to his office. As the elevator doors opened, I saw him sitting at the conference room table, engaged in a business meeting. I momentarily caught his eye. I walked past the conference door and straight to his office. He quickly followed me in and shut the door behind him. Immediately, he could tell that something was terribly wrong and I launched into what had just transpired only a few minutes before. In his loving and gentle way, he assured me that everything was going to be okay and that we didn't need to be worried. He reminded me that we didn't have the results from the biopsy yet and, most likely, they would come back with a favorable outcome. He let me vent, cry, and pace for a little while. Once he could see that I had calmed down a bit, we agreed that we would talk more about it when he got home from work. But even in his strength, I could see he was frightened, too.

I'm typically a pretty positive person, and I try to look for the good in every situation. I make a conscious effort to not dwell on the worst-case scenario or let my mind take a nosedive into "Oh, crap land," and this was no exception. But as I went back home and entered the house, I could feel a shift in the air. The piles of laundry that needed to be put away and the dishes in the sink, all of a sudden, didn't have the urgency lights flashing over them like earlier in the day. Everything felt a little heavier and what was a normal house when I left that morning, seemed a little dark and stale. In spite of my traditionally upbeat self; I was scared.

I also had a very distinct feeling in my heart that was telling me the biopsy was going to come back with less than ideal results. It wasn't a sinking, horrible, panicky gut feeling, but more of a gentle knowing. Don't get me wrong. I was still terrified and feeling like I wanted to scream, but I believe God was preparing me for the news I would soon receive. He was being a loving Father by giving me just a little foreknowledge to slightly soften the blow. Even through my weakness and my fear, His peace, which transcends all understanding, was guarding my heart and mind. This would be a pattern that I would see as my journey continued and just one of the examples of how God was gently leading me by the hand through this nightmare.

6

Happy Distraction

"I say to myself, "The Lord is my portion; therefore I will wait for him."
Lamentations 3:24

During the five days that we waited for the results, we thankfully had a much more joyous occasion to keep our minds occupied. Andrew's younger cousin was getting married, and the happy couple had asked him to officiate the wedding. Not being a pastor by trade, this was a first for him, and as I helped him prepare for the ceremony, we dove into what makes a strong marriage and how to communicate that in a way that would bless not only the couple but also the guests in attendance.

We were current, living examples of the trials that couples face, and here we had an opportunity to focus, not on ourselves, but on how we could serve another couple. We poured all of our energy, not into our current drama, but into loving and supporting them. However, it wasn't always easy. We chose to put on brave, happy faces, celebrated and danced, all while keeping our secret to ourselves while wondering if our world was crashing around us as two beautiful people were having the happiest moment of their lives. But we kept everything to ourselves because it wasn't the time to share. There would be plenty of time to do that later. Being surrounded by family, even though they had no idea what was happening, was so comforting.

Throughout that long weekend, we were strong on the outside during the day, but once we were in the privacy of our hotel room in the evenings, we let our guards down and were real with each other. We shared our feelings, anxieties, our tears, and pressed into God through praying together and reading our Bible.

One of my daily routines that I love to do every morning is to spend some time with God either in prayer, reading my Bible, meditating, or all of the above. Some mornings are a little crazier than others and, on those days, when I find I only have a few minutes, I like to read *Jesus Calling* by Sarah Young. It's a daily devotional that gives me bite-sized chunks of encouragement that I can chew on, put in my pocket, and think about as I get my day started. Knowing I wouldn't have any definitive answers about the biopsy for almost five days, I was struggling with the agony of the waiting game. So, to help combat that, I opened my Bible more and made checking my daily devotion a priority.

When we draw closer to God, He will draw closer to us. This promise became a beautiful reality to me in those early days of uncertainty. During those agonizing moments of waiting for my results, He led me to Lamentations 3:21-26 and 57. *"Yet this I will call to mind and therefore I have hope: Because of the Lord's great love we are not consumed, for his compassions never fail. They are new every morning; great is your faithfulness. I say to myself, 'The Lord is my portion; therefore, I will wait for him.' The Lord is good to those whose hope is in him, to the one who seeks him; it is good to wait quietly for the salvation of the Lord.... You came near when I called you, and you said, 'Do not fear.'"*

Four very distinct pieces of these verses jumped out at me. The first was "hope." When we are faced with tragedy, major uncertainty, or an extreme trial, the first emotion we often feel is hopelessness. It's very easy to find ourselves sinking into a pit of despair and to feel as though there is no way out. Our mind goes to the worst-case scenario, and we think there is nothing, or no one, who can help get us out of where we are at the time.

The word, hope, is thrown around a lot, almost like a life preserver that's tossed to someone sinking in the ocean. But if that life preserver isn't tied to a rope which is attached to a live person who can pull us into a safe boat, it will do us no good. There has to be something tangible on the other side of that life preserver that can actually help us and bring us to a safe place. For me, that certainty on the other end of my rope was the "Lord's, great love." But to have that hope I had to grab that life preserver and hold on for dear life. I couldn't simply touch it or slip it around my body for a few minutes. No, I had to hold on with both hands and make the conscious decision not to let go, no matter what.

The second part of those verses that spoke to me was the Lord's unwavering faithfulness. When Andrew and I were married, one of the songs that we chose to have sung at our wedding was the hymn, "Great is Thy Faithfulness." The chorus of this beautiful song begins with "Great is Thy faithfulness, great is Thy faithfulness, morning by morning new mercies I see." The promises of this song that were sung over us as a newly married couple ten years ago were being brought back in a whole different context, and God was beginning to set the stage for me as I entered into this frightful and unknown territory. When God promises to be faithful, He is committing to be consistent and unchangeable. God will keep His promises, and we can solidly trust in Him. God was teaching me to give Him all of my fears and to believe that He would faithfully see me through.

The third truth that hit me like a ton of bricks, or what I like to refer to as a God "two-by-four upside the head," was when He told me, through those verses, to "wait," and not just to wait, but to wait quietly. So, darn it, that meant I was supposed to be still, not run around like a wild maniac or start telling everyone my sky was falling and get the drama pot all stirred up. This is hard to do. I'll be honest, often times my first reaction when "you know what" is hitting the fan is to call my mom and dad, or my best friend, and unload like a crazy woman. But God was telling me to wait quietly, and that was what I was going to have to do. Now, did I still call my parents and my best friend? Heck, yes, I did! But over the next five days, while anxious for any definitive answers on my biopsy, I waited quietly and kept everything to myself.

Lastly, God gave me the words in those verses that I really needed to hear. "Do not fear." His reassuring voice gave me the strength to get out of bed, face the next few days, and to keep putting one foot in front of the other. Knowing the course of my life could change drastically was terrifying, but every time I felt myself getting crippled by that uncertainty, I kept repeating those words in my head. It gave me just enough of what I needed to make it past each minute and each hour as they slowly ticked closer and closer to what I knew was coming.

7

Monday

"You are my hiding place; you will protect me from trouble and surround me with songs of deliverance."
Psalm 32:7

It was here. I was both dreading and looking forward to this day. Monday. The day I could expect the phone call that would either take this nightmare away or send my family and our world into a tailspin. I didn't know exactly when the call would come, so I went about our routine as usual; kids up, kids dressed, breakfast on the table, teeth brushed, backpacks on and out the door. I went on with my day, ran a few errands, and tried to make the time feel as normal as possible. But inside I was in agony. I didn't know when the call would come, and every time my phone rang, I shuttered. First, it was the cable repairman confirming our appointment that morning, then it was the random telemarketing call. Finally, at four o'clock in the afternoon, it rang again, and this time the caller ID confirmed it was the hospital.

My heart began to pound, and I made a point to sit down before I answered the call. I put the phone to my ear and heard my radiologist's voice on the other end. She got right to the point. She didn't preface it with much as she said what I already knew in my heart she would say.

"You have breast cancer."

It's funny. As soon as I heard those words, I didn't cry. Instead, my mind kicked into clinical mode. I asked questions and lots of them. I wanted to know what the next step was and what I needed to do. I wanted as much information as I could possibly have so I grabbed the closest piece of paper I could find as I frantically wrote down everything she said. She didn't have a lot of details because we were in the very early stages of my diagnosis, but she asked if I was free to meet with the surgeon the next day. Um, yeah. I'm definitely free. My schedule just got cleared by a bulldozer. We made the appointment for the following afternoon, and I hung up the phone.

Without even releasing the phone from my hand, I dialed my husband's number, and it barely rang two times. He answered, and I said, "I have cancer." He replied with, "I'm on my way home," and he hung up. Immediately there was knock on the back door, and flustered, I walked down the hall to open it. It was my sweet neighbor and her daughters selling something for a school fundraiser. I couldn't tell you what it was or what I bought, but I remember shoving $20 at them and thinking, "You have no idea what is happening to me." It felt so bizarre knowing that life was going on around me as usual, children were raising money for their school, people were heading to the gym to workout, moms were doing laundry somewhere, but my life had been completely knocked off the rails, and I wanted to explode. I smiled at them and engaged in a little small talk, but it took all that I had inside me to keep from ugly crying all over them.

After they left, I busied myself with preparing dinner and waiting for Andrew to get home. When he arrived, we quickly retreated to another room and discussed our plan for how and when we were going to tell the girls the news. We decided that there was no better time than right now. We knew we wanted to be as open and honest with them as possible.

Being six and seven and a half years old, at the time, we understood the need to be careful with the way we presented the information to them, but we also knew that it was important for us to include them in the process. I began to tell them that I had seen the doctor a few days ago because I had found a lump in my breast. Then I said to them that the doctor had called me to give me the news that I had breast cancer. Lauren, my oldest, blurted out with a smile and a bit of excitement, "You have cancer just like my friend's mom!" I was honestly taken back a little by her flippant, almost joyful reaction, but then I realized her thought process as a child. She was relating my diagnosis to my friend's similar and recent diagnosis which was now public knowledge at her school. Now Lauren had something in common with this other mother's child and fellow classmate.

I confirmed that, yes, there were two mommies now at her school that had breast cancer, but then we shared that this wasn't something to be happy or excited about. It was a challenge finding a way to share the information in a sobering manner so that they would understand the gravity of it, and yet keep the discussion positive and upbeat as not to frighten them. We talked about the similarities between her and her classmate, and how they could support each other. We focused on what a blessing it was that they could do that and that they weren't alone in what we were all going to be facing together.

As we talked, Andrew and I walked that fine line of being transparent regarding the serious nature of this disease, and still staying optimistic. I didn't want the girls to feel scared or, at this point, to even know that cancer can be fatal. We explained to them that we were in the early stages of figuring out my treatment plan and that it was going to be a long and hard road for all of us. We let them know that they may see Daddy and Mommy cry at times, or even laugh, and all of those emotions are normal. But most importantly, we explained to them that we were trusting God to heal me, and we were leaning on Him for support and strength as we began this journey together. We knew the importance of modeling our faith in this very real situation and actively living out Psalm 46:1-3. *"God is our refuge and strength, a very present help in trouble. Therefore, we will not fear though the earth gives way, though the mountains be moved into the heart of the sea, though its waters roar and foam, though the mountains tremble at its swelling."*

8

I Need to Get Away

"You will keep in perfect peace those whose minds are steadfast, because they trust in you."
Isaiah 26:3

After sharing the news with my closest family and friends, I made it more public with a post on my Facebook page. I actually did this more for other people than myself. I knew the news would spread and I didn't want my friends to feel uncomfortable about talking with me about it. I wanted to avoid that awkward moment of interaction when you know they know, but they don't know if they should say anything or much less what to say. I thought that making everything more public would help alleviate that weirdness for us all. I essentially wanted to hand out permission slips for others to approach the elephant in the room. My hope for my post was to be honest, transparent, and real with where my head and heart were. A very simple announcement flowed out in about 20 minutes after sitting in front of my computer, and it felt both liberating and terrifying when I finally found the courage to click, "share."

I am the one in eight. A few days ago, I was diagnosed with breast cancer. In this country, one in eight women will be diagnosed with this disease. I am the typical, young, healthy woman who does not have a significant family history of this particular disease. I have annual mammograms and my most recent one this past November came back clean. However, about a month ago I felt a small lump in my breast. As most mothers do, I put off taking care of myself, and I didn't address it until last week when my friend told me she was diagnosed with breast cancer. After that conversation, I immediately drove home and called my doctor, and here we are.

Right now, I am trusting Jesus every moment and taking things one step at a time. He has given me such PEACE and confirmation that He is walking right alongside me through this trial that I WILL overcome. He continues to impress upon my heart that in this world we will have trouble, but He has overcome the world. (John 16:33). My prayer is that He be glorified through this process and that I may learn the true measure of trusting Him. I know He's not through with me yet. I know He has a plan and a purpose for my life, as He does for all of us. He is my rock and my salvation, and in the end, we WIN!

Some have been asking how they can help. TRULY, the only thing we are asking for at this time is PRAYER. Prayer for healing, prayer for our girls, prayer for wisdom for the doctors, and prayer for strength through this process. Women, please be diligent about your annual breast exams, and if you find something that seems off, get it checked immediately. I can't stress enough how important that is. Even if you think, "I'm healthy! I'm young! This could never happen to me!" It doesn't matter. I thought the same thing.

So, even though I felt that I had a pretty extensive life experience "resume" so far, I guess I will be adding this to this list...

BREAST CANCER SURVIVOR

Let the fight begin.

After being hit with this crazy news and finally letting the cat out of the bag, all I wanted to do was get away and process everything. My mind was completely racing with every possible scenario, spotty pieces of information that we were slowly gathering during these initial stages, and a whirlwind of emotions. Thankfully, God knew exactly what we needed as a family and, coincidently, or not, we had a long weekend planned in Chicago that couldn't have come at a better time.

We packed our suitcases and jumped on the train armed with stuffed animals, coloring books, and a huge carry-on bag of cut veggies, fruits, and nuts. My husband, the constant researcher, had begun scouring books and websites on healthy eating and anti-cancer diets.

Approximately two months before my diagnosis, we were at a leadership conference in Florida among other attendees from all over the country. During dinner one evening, we randomly sat down at one of the round tables with other people we had never met. We all went around the table introducing ourselves and shared basic personal, ice-breaker-type information. The young couple sitting next to us began sharing their story and proceeded to tell us that the wife was a cancer survivor. They shared how they felt very strongly about fighting her cancer using diet change and I found myself absolutely fascinated by her story. Keep in mind this was before I had any inkling that I would be in her shoes in just a few short months, but I was firmly and strangely drawn to everything she was saying. I was taking mental notes and decided that night that I was going to adapt some of her practices just because I thought it sounded interesting and very healthy. I believe this was another situation where God was preparing me for my future, and that it was not a coincidence that we sat next to this particular couple that evening.

Now cancer was MY reality. Andrew and I began reflecting on the information we learned from this couple, and we started following her blog, anticancermom.com. We too decided that we would make some drastic changes in our eating habits and that I would be very diligent about how I fueled my body before, during, and after treatment. We decided on a hybrid diet that consisted of primarily organic vegetables, fruits, nuts, whole grains, wild caught salmon, and eggs. We decreased our dairy intake, and I eliminated processed sugar altogether. We added protein-packed smoothies and a lot of vegetable juicing.

I realize that there are many opinions on what the proper diet is for fighting disease, but this was what felt right for us, so it's what we chose to do. When you're faced with a physical condition that you feel completely at the mercy of, there is a terrifying sense of having no control over your body.

Being able to take specific steps regarding my diet was an area where I felt I had some control. We knew we would be incorporating traditional medicine into my treatment, but my food became a partner in the process. It was a small part, but it made me feel like I actually had a hand in my healing, and it became my way of fighting back. It released me from the feeling of helplessness to feeling helpful.

Those first couple of days were very difficult as I adjusted to my new diet. Granted, it was even worse because we were traveling, and I didn't have the comfort of my own kitchen to prepare what I needed and wanted to eat. I became what you'd call "hangry." I was hungry, and I was angry because I couldn't eat what was familiar and easy to me. I missed my comfort foods, and there were moments when I would have agreed to do a jig on a busy street corner in a rainbow tutu for a slice of gooey, cheesy pizza and a chocolate malt with extra whipped cream. Thank goodness for that enormous stash of snacks we brought with us. I pretty much lived with my head in that bag between meals as I figured out what I could consume next. I then carefully, and painstakingly, navigated restaurant menus while driving the waiters and waitress crazy with my endless questions.

After I identified the one vegetarian, maybe even slightly vegan option on the buffet at the hotel, we settled in to try and enjoy these few days of escape. That was exactly what it was, an escape. I was running away from the reality of what was happening and taking solace in a completely different environment. There was something very comforting about that because it allowed me to take my focus off of my day to day normal responsibilities and to press into God and process my reality. We spent time doing fun things with the girls like exploring the Shedd Aquarium, the Chicago Children's Museum, the Adler Planetarium during the day, and in the evenings, Andrew let me sneak away to a quiet area of the hotel lounge to read, research my diagnosis, pray, and write.

One morning I decided to spend a little time in the hotel gym, which is a place you would have never found me in the past while on a vacation, but this time was different. I had read about the importance of regular exercise and how it boosts your immune system, so the running shoes went on, the earbuds went in, and I introduced myself to my new best friend, the treadmill.

We were staying at a hotel in the heart of Chicago and, true to most hotels in a large city, our room and the gym were on the upper levels of a beautiful high-rise building. When I walked into the gym, I spotted a row of treadmills lined up like daunting metal soldiers placed against a massive wall of floor-to-ceiling windows. I fired one up, started walking, and cranked up my contemporary Christian playlist in my earbuds. The first song that came on was one by Jeremy Camp called "Same Power." The lyrics that poured into my head and settled into my heart were powerful.

I can walk, down this dark and painful road
I can face
Every fear of the unknown
I can hear
All God's children singing out
We will not be overtaken
We will not be overcome
The same power that rose Jesus from the grave
The same power that commands the dead to wake
Lives in us, lives in us
The same power that moves mountains when He speaks
The same power that can calm a raging sea
Lives in us, lives in us
He lives in us, lives in us

I could feel myself breathe and finally exhale the breath I had been holding so tightly these past few days. The song was a beautiful reminder that, yes, this cancer was physically in me, but guess what, cancer, so is the Holy Spirit! 1 John 4:4 says, "*Little children, you are from God and have overcome them, for He who is in you is greater than he who is in the world.*" An image came to mind of a battle raging inside of me, but the best news was that this battle was not one-sided. Yes, I had a hostile adversary, but there was also a faithful and all-powerful ally that was standing in the same ring with bigger boxing gloves and way stronger muscles. I was rooting for that guy, and I knew at that moment that I had to keep cheering Him on, believing that He would throw the heavy punches for me.

As I continued to walk at the mercy of the treadmill, I started to feel very strongly that I was to be open and vulnerable with my journey and to share the good, the bad, and the ugly. I struggled with that, however, because I struggle with putting myself out there. There are things I would rather keep private and would much prefer to live under the radar. I think I'm similar to a lot of women who have a fear of judgment from others and who struggle with the need for approval. I was afraid to be bold and talk about my faith because I didn't want to annoy people or seem like that crazy religious girl that so often turns people off. As I turned up the speed on my treadmill, I started praying. I asked God to help me understand at what level I was to share my faith and quite simply, what I should do.

The answer He gave me was profound. He used my surroundings to speak very loudly and very clearly to what His direction was for me. I looked out from where I was and from this high vantage point in the city, up against a wall of windows, I saw just that. Thousands and thousands of windows symmetrically placed on all of the tall buildings surrounded me. All I could see were windows, and there was a gentle impression in my heart that said, "I want you to be a window for others to see Me."

That was it. A simple and yet straightforward answer. I knew the path I was to take with this, and that path was allowing myself to be exposed. God was giving me the opportunity to use my pain to give Him glory and just as that treadmill had me as an active but captive participant, I couldn't walk away from that.

9

What's the Plan?

"What's the plan?" If you asked my parents, they would confirm that even as a child I always needed to know the plan. I'm that type of person that functions best with structure and a good dose of certainty. Tell me to pack my bags with a swimsuit and a pair of good walking shoes and not tell me where we are going, while exciting and fun, secretly sends me into a slight inner panic. "What if I need different walking shoes or I need an active swimming suit versus a cute, beach chair lounging, fruity drink sipping swimming suit?" So, being in this current, slow, and laborious stage of determining my treatment plan was rough for all of us.

It takes time to get all the information that you need to put together the best treatment plan, and frequently you are presented with options and lots of them. This makes it even more difficult because there comes a time when you just want someone to tell you what to do. I didn't want to be left to make my own decision for fear of making the wrong one. But physicians are typically really good about doing their job which is to give you the information, share their recommendations, but then give you the authority to choose what you feel is best for you. This is the hard part.

At this point, we had determined a few key pieces of information. I had a clinical stage one, grade three, invasive ductal breast carcinoma, and the tumor was a little over one centimeter in diameter. Immunohisto-chemistry testing of the tumor revealed the breast cancer cells did not express estrogen or progesterone receptors. Additionally, a separate receptor, HER2, was not overexpressed by the breast cancer cells. You're probably thinking, "I have no earthly clue what she is talking about, and this might as well be Chinese." Funny, we thought the same thing. When you are diagnosed with this crazy disease, you begin to learn way more about it than you ever wanted to know. Over time, you find yourself speaking this weird "cancerese" that only you and the people close to you understand. So, I'll try to break it down for you a bit.

Specific cells in our bodies, including cancer cells, have receptors that gather information from things in our bloodstream. These receptors then tell the cells what to do or not to do. It's similar to putting a key into your car ignition. If the key fits and turns the ignition the car will start. Normal breast tissue cells have a receptor that is a hormone receptor, and these receptors are like little beacons for the hormone's estrogen and/or progesterone. These hormones help with the basic functions of breast cells. Having all three of these receptors come back as negative, as in my case, is not as common and is considered a rarer subtype of breast cancer. The most common subtype is hormone receptor-positive, HER2 negative. So, it was determined that the breast cancer I was dealing with was ER/PR (estrogen and progesterone) negative and HER2 negative. HER2 stands for human epidermal growth factor receptor 2. It is also a receptor that when you know the status of, it can help determine treatment. For example, if the breast cancer is hormone receptor-positive, then endocrine therapy is a potential treatment option. Similarly, if the HER2 receptor is positive then an additional drug, Herceptin, is an additional treatment option.

So, long story short, my cancer was what they call "triple negative." Coming from a past extensive dance background I thought, "Oh cool! That's kind of like a triple threat (a performer who is fantastic at dancing, acting, and singing)!" Yeah, well, not so much. Now I was part of the 25% of women diagnosed with triple negative breast cancer, and I was dealing with a triple threat, but it definitely wasn't the feel good, Gene Kelly, Broadway-show-type.

The other piece of information that we needed to wait for was the genetic testing. We met with the genetic counselor, and she was wonderful. She explained what the BRCA1 and BRCA2 gene mutations were and that she was going to test me for these two particular mutations as well as some additional ones that could be present. This would be helpful information, not only for determining my treatment, but also for my daughters to know as they got older. It would give them valuable information regarding whether or not they were potential carriers of the gene and at a higher risk for breast cancer as well as other types of cancers themselves.

We were told that we would have to wait one to three weeks for the results of those tests so once again we were in a holding pattern. It felt like we were on an airplane and the pilot had just come over the intercom to say, "Ladies and gentlemen, there is a nasty storm brewing over our destination so we will be circling over the airport for the next three hours." Really? The delays in getting answers were brutal. We knew it was necessary, but emotionally it was excruciating.

One of the big, scary questions still looming was if I was going to require chemotherapy. Obviously, I was hoping that I would be spared this particular treatment which I knew could be very harsh and difficult. Even before my diagnosis, I was very conscious about avoiding potentially toxic chemicals in general and had been making an effort to decrease our family's exposure to them as much as possible. So, the thought of pumping strong drugs like chemo through my veins absolutely terrified me.

As a woman, I also had a fear of the side effects, both internally and externally. Losing my hair and potentially my eyelashes and eyebrows was a sobering thought, and I wrestled with that possibility quite a bit. But once again, God began preparing me for this potential reality. One evening before bed, I opened my Bible and it fell open to Ezekiel chapter five. The first part of verse one says, *"Now, son of man, take a sharp sword and use it as a barber's razor to shave your head and your beard."* That verse might as well have been a neon sign on a billboard with blinking arrows pointing to it. As much as I didn't like what I was feeling in my heart, I knew God was trying to tell me that I was going to be losing my hair and that chemotherapy was definitely in my future. This wasn't one of those, "Whoo hoo, God! Thanks so much for the revelation!" No, it was more of a sad knowing that I was actually going to be facing this harsh reality. I was grateful for the foreknowledge and thankful for a God who loves me enough to soften the blow for me, but at the same time, I was crushed.

We continued to busy ourselves during this time of uncertainty and dove head first into one of the few things we could control -- that diet thing! Now that we were on this new healthy eating kick, we decided to stockpile fresh vegetable juices and not only that, we were going to juice them ourselves. We gathered some recipes from our new cancer survivor friend who we met in Florida, loaded the kids up in the car, and descended upon the organic produce department at our local grocery store. When I tell you we cleaned out the entire organic section, I mean we seriously cleaned it out. It was a little ridiculous. Pushing two full carts of broccoli, carrots, beets, ginger, cucumbers, and green apples, we caravanned down the store aisles like we were heading to feed a compound of rabbits. Once we got home and unloaded the mounds of bags, we realized we had underestimated our juicing capabilities and needed reinforcements.

A desperate call went out to our close group of friends that we affectionately call our "Life Group." These four couples are gems of humanity that we have been meeting with on a regular basis for years. We laugh together, cry together, and, most importantly, study God's Word and pray together. The need for some vegetable cleaners, choppers, and juicers was explained, and in a matter of hours, a juicing extravaganza was planned. We all took turns in the assembly line, prepping and running the electric juicer, and ultimately, tasting each individual concoction in shot glasses. Some were met with puckered lips and hesitant, wordless nods, and some got smiles and rave reviews. All in all, it was a success, and we canned and froze a healthy stash of what one of our friends affectionately called, "Godka."

Once the vegetable carnage was cleaned up in our friend's kitchen, we sat down and shared our hearts and the struggles we were having with deciding on a plan. We still had a few pieces of information we were waiting on regarding the traditional medicine option, but Andrew was also feeling strongly about looking into alternative methods. We ended the night with them praying for us, as my heart cried out for answers. I was so thankful for these beautiful people and their wisdom and friendship. The next morning, one of these friends sent me a text quoting Isaiah 30:21 that spoke directly to our need for a clear path: "*Whether you turn to the right or to the left, your ears will hear a voice behind you, saying, "This is the way; walk in it."*

10

Still Waters

"From the ends of the earth I call to you, I call as my heart grows faint; lead me to the rock that is higher than I. For you have been my refuge, a strong tower against the foe. I long to dwell in your tent forever and take refuge in the shelter of your wings."
Psalm 61: 2-4

The days continued to tick by slowly, and while I had received the good news that my genetic testing had come back negative confirming that I didn't have the gene mutation, we were still waiting on MRI results that would give us more information on the actual size of the tumor. This was the big missing piece to the puzzle we had been spending all of this time trying to fit together. Once we knew the MRI findings, we would be presented with the treatment scenarios and would finally be able to make a decision. Then we could get this show on the road. The anticipation was high, and we were emotionally tired.

We had weekend plans to travel to my parent's cabin on a lake in northern Wisconsin for some much-needed time with the family. We made efforts to keep the mood as light as possible for the girls and to enjoy the time with my parents. Knowing my surgeon would be calling over the weekend with my results, we gave him the phone number to the cabin, and we waited. There was a constant, slight feeling of tension that hung in the air as the minutes and hours ticked by. Even over the laughter when my Dad got walloped by my daughter in UNO, and when we happily prepared meals in the kitchen, the anticipation was always there. Then the phone rang.

I answered the call and heard my surgeon's voice on the other end of the line. The news was not great. The tumor was slightly larger than we initially thought and there were a couple of questionable areas on my left breast which had originally been the unaffected side. I had the call on speaker phone, so everyone could hear. Because of the size of the tumor, my physician was definitely recommending chemotherapy. Even though I already had a feeling this news was coming, my heart sank.

I needed to walk. I needed to get out of the house and process my feelings. Andrew and I left the girls with my parents, and we started walking down the Northwoods road. I felt defeated as though I had just taken a big fat blow to the stomach. I thought for sure the news would be better or at least be nothing new. I wasn't expecting it to be worse. As we walked down the road, we didn't say much but listened to the wind in the pines and slowly breathed in the fresh air. The skies were slightly overcast completely mirroring what I was feeling inside. With each step, we got closer to one of our favorite little ponds. It's a picturesque small body of water right off the road surrounded by beautiful pine and oak trees. Psalm 23 kept running over and over in my mind and, more specifically, the first few verses. *"The Lord is my Shepherd, I lack nothing. He makes me lie down in green pastures, he leads me beside quiet waters, he refreshes my soul. He guides me along the right paths for his name's sake. Even though I walk through the darkest valley, I will fear no evil, for you are with me..."*

As those verses played over and over in my head like a skipping record, we walked around the bend and the pond came into view. We stopped and sat down next to the edge of the water. Again, those verses repeated themselves. *"...he leads me beside still waters..."* I looked out over the water, and it was indeed completely still. Not a ripple or wave to be seen.

Even though my insides were in turmoil, I was feeling the quietness of God right here in His creation. He was reminding me that even though I did not have the answers, I did not have my health, and I did not have much certainty, I still "lacked nothing." He was refreshing my soul by quiet waters and gently comforting me through my pain. I began to realize how important it was that I continue to keep my eyes and my mind open to Him at all times. He was using His Word and nature to show His love for me at that moment, and all I needed to do was receive it.

After returning home from our walk, we looked out at the large lake in front of our house. This lake has a lot of open water, and the winds and breezes are fairly constant in this particular area. However, this time the water was like glass. Similar to the pond we were just sitting near, this body of water was also completely still. I could see the reflection of the clouds on the surface, and the horizon seemed to melt into the lake as though it were one continuous piece. We all remarked at how utterly rare this was, and we couldn't remember the last time it was this still. Coincidence? I don't think so. I felt so drawn to the peace that was coming off that lake that Andrew and I immediately walked down to the water's edge, got in our kayaks, and began gliding and quietly cutting through the stillness of the surface. I rejoiced in my heart for confirmation that even though my life felt like a hurricane, God was telling me that He was truly going to lead me beside His still waters.

That evening, I tried to sleep but woke up in the middle of the night extremely restless. I was hungry, frustrated, and feeling overwhelming stress. With chemo looming in my future, I began worrying about how I was going to manage the hair loss. Questions were swirling in my head. "Do I cut my hair? If so, how short do I go? Do I leave it and just let it all fall out? Or do I completely shave it? If so, when?" The voices were tormenting me, so I got up and went into the living room to pray. I sat in the dark on the couch, and a dim, almost ghostly light coming through the picture window facing the lake filled the room. The stars were trying to peek out from the clouds but struggling to do so and the diffused grayish blue hue reflecting off the water made the room feel eerily still and spectral. Even with my family sleeping just steps away, I felt very alone.

I began praying softly. As I prayed, I felt an overwhelming sorrow come over me. An image of Jesus praying in the Garden of Gethsemane the night before his crucifixion came into my mind and for an instant, I felt like I was at that place. By no means was my situation anything like what Jesus endured, but I think He was bringing this image into my mind as a way to show me that He understood my pain. He too faced death, isolation, many questions, and fear. Jesus prayed that His Father would "remove this cup from" Him. He prayed that He wouldn't have to go through the agony of a criminal's death, but He also prayed that God's will would be done and that no matter what happened that it would not be what Jesus wanted, but what His Father wanted.

I quietly cried as the shadows of the trees outside made strange patterns on the living room floor, and after a few more minutes, I felt my heart slightly settle. I opened my devotional book. By the light of the small lamp next to the couch, I read the entry for that day. It was Exodus 33:14, and it said, *"The Lord replied, "My Presence will go with you, and I will give you rest."* I closed my book and went back to bed.

11

The Decision

"Whoever dwells in the shelter of the Most High will rest in the shadow of the Almighty. I will say of the Lord, "He is my refuge and my fortress, my God, in whom I trust."
Psalm 91:1-2

It was time to meet with my oncologist, and she confirmed that yes, I would need to have a series of chemotherapy treatments. We were finally at that stage where all of the information we needed to make a treatment plan had been gathered, and now it was up to us to choose which plan we wanted to go with. Andrew and I were in a full-blown stage of mental medical fatigue at this point. The countless trips to the hospital for tests, test results, mountains of information downloads and more tests were wearing on both of us. Our minds were swirling, and I was tired of being poked and prodded. We were emotionally drained.

My oncologist and surgeon both recommended that I have four to six chemo treatments and a mastectomy. I could choose between having a single mastectomy or a prophylactic double mastectomy. I also had the choice of doing the chemo before surgery or after surgery. At this point, it didn't look like I would need to have radiation based on the ultrasound findings, and thankfully my lymph nodes were looking clear of cancer. However, we wouldn't know for sure until after the mastectomy surgery when the lymph node biopsy would be performed.

All of the potential side-effects of the chemo treatments were laid out for us, and honestly, it was a little terrifying. Doctors, being the wonderful medical professionals that they are, are required to give you the full scoop straight up, but as the onslaught of potential risks kept coming, I could feel both Andrew and I slowly sink into our chairs like ice cream melting on a hot day. We took copious notes and tried to absorb all of the information into our already saturated brains.

We left the appointment with a day or two to discuss and decide on what we were going to do. I could tell that Andrew was pretty shaken up by all he had heard, and he was wrestling with the thought of me having to go through it all. He was worried about my body, the potential short and long-term side-effects, and how that would impact both of our lives moving forward. He was afraid, and his very normal tendency to want to "fix-it" kicked into high gear.

Because God had been preparing me for this particular treatment path that included chemotherapy, I had peace, but unfortunately, that was not the case with my husband. We went to bed that evening, and around two o'clock in the morning I rolled over and noticed that he wasn't lying next to me. I immediately jumped out of bed and went downstairs in search of him. I found him in our dark office with his face lit only by the soft blue glow from the computer screen.

He was scouring the internet for alternatives and answers to the many questions that were plaguing him. He was fighting the chemotherapy option with everything in him and hoping and praying that he could come up with a better, less drastic, solution. I stood at the corner of the desk, tired, and slightly annoyed because I already knew what my path was going to be. Mentally I was in a place where I wanted to make the decision and get on with executing the plan, but Andrew was nowhere near that same point. As much as I wanted to scream and shake him for dragging this out,

I knew he needed to go through this process to come to the same conclusion that I had, on his own. I was frustrated, but I was also filled with such a deep love for this man that cared this much about me and our family that he would try anything to protect me.

I stood in the dark by the corner of the desk with my head in my hands, weeping, as I tried to explain to him that I just wanted to make a decision and move forward. The information gathering and waiting process was taking its toll, and I was done fighting this process. Despite my pleas, he said he wanted to explore one more option before we made our final decision. During this time, we had been talking with the same couple we met a few months prior who gave us the very helpful information about diet, and they recommended a physician at a medical center in the South who was an integrative oncologist. The integrative approach combines modern medicine with natural medicine. Some patients have found success with this method of treatment and I firmly believe that every cancer case is unique. As a patient, you have to decide which plan is right for you, and I can't say that one is better or worse than the other. I simply don't have that knowledge base, but I do believe it's important to do your research and ask a lot of questions when you're going through this decision-making process.

Andrew really wanted to explore this alternative choice and asked if we could set up a call to talk to one of the physicians at this center. I agreed because I respected the process that Andrew had to go through to get to the final outcome. I knew he needed to exhaust these options or he would always wonder and doubt. The "what ifs" would always plague him and I knew that neither he nor I could live with that. My hope and prayer was that in the end, we would be on the same page and united when it came time for us to make that decision. I needed him on my side to help me confidently walk this journey out.

Andrew arranged the call for the following day, and I met him at his office. He closed the door and turned on the speakerphone. He went through his extensive list of questions with the physician on the other end of the line, and I listened. I had a few questions, but I still knew where my heart was as I asked them. If we chose the integrative oncology route, it would require that I stay at the center for weeks or potentially months at a time. I would be many miles away from my home, family, and my support network, and honestly, that frightened me.

I realize that sometimes it's necessary to travel and stay somewhere far from home to get the care that you need or want, and again everyone's situation is different, but for me, I couldn't stand the thought of leaving my daughters. I knew that I wanted my girls to watch me go through this and to be a part of this journey. I knew that I needed my parents as support and that they needed to feel like they could help me, too. I couldn't put that kind of distance between myself, my family, and the other friends who I knew would surround me with their love. I still had this feeling deep inside that I was supposed to face this trial and the traditional chemotherapy treatments and all of the unknowns and fears that come with it. I couldn't explain why, but I just knew.

After all of the questions had been asked and Andrew's computer screen was full of notes, he hung up the phone. He looked at me across his desk with excited and expectant eyes, and I could tell he liked everything he had heard. He said, "Well, what do you think?" I paused for a moment, looked at him and said, "Honey, it's not for me." His face fell, and I could tell he was absolutely defeated. He could see that I had made up my mind. I explained that I wanted to stay home and do the traditional medicine route at the local hospital where I felt comfortable and safe. I shared the peace that God had been giving me about this decision and that I felt very strongly about this path. I truly believed that this was what I was supposed to do and that part of this plan would include some intense chemotherapy treatments. Andrew's eyes lowered, and he could see that I had made up my mind.

The next night we met with our Life Group friends. We sat around the kitchen table and gave them an update. We told them that we had decided on my treatment plan and I began explaining what that would be. I shared that it would consist of four to six rounds of chemotherapy followed by a double mastectomy and reconstruction. It didn't look like I would need radiation, but this would be determined after surgery and the findings of the lymph node biopsy.

At this point, I was feeling a slight feeling of relief because we now had a plan and could openly share it. So, I rattled off the bits of information that we knew at this point. As I was talking, I started hearing some slight sniffles, and I turned to look toward Andrew's direction. He put his head in his hands and began to cry. The crying turned into weeping, and his shoulders started convulsing as the tears flowed and began soaking his shirt sleeves. He laid his head on his folded arms and slumped over the table sobbing. It caught me off guard because I hadn't seen him get quite this emotional since this all started. Yes, we had cried together multiple times after the original diagnosis, but this was a release of emotions that hadn't happened yet, and it was coming like a flood. The other four men at the table immediately got up and surrounded him. They took him into another part of the kitchen and left us ladies at the table. They let him talk, vent, cry, and they listened, put their hands on his shoulders and prayed.

This was his breaking moment. The realization that he couldn't fix my cancer and the complete lack of control over the outcome was crushing him. He was afraid for his wife, and he was finally at a place where he had to take his hands off the wheel and release the love of his life to the Lord. He had to trust that God would protect me, and he had to surrender. He had to stop trying to do it all himself and give up striving to have all the answers. He needed to lay this disease at the feet of Jesus and simply trust that God's plan was better than his. This was the place that Andrew needed to get to for multiple reasons.

As a couple, we needed to be united in our game plan moving forward, and Andrew needed to be in a place of surrender to allow God to really work in his heart. Even though Andrew couldn't see it at that moment, God was releasing the burden from him by showing him that he couldn't do this on his own. In fact, it wasn't Andrew's job to heal me or have all of the answers, and the weight of that heavy responsibility that he was putting on himself was crushing him.

So, as the tears flowed, the same peace that I had felt weeks before, began to slowly permeate in him and mingle with his immense sadness. But we were finally there. By Andrew voicing his feelings and realizing what God was showing him, we were finally on the same page.

The next morning, the Lord impressed upon Andrew's heart these words: "When are you going to trust Me with your wife? Look at what I have done in caring for you, your daughters, and your business. Trust Me that I have her. She is My daughter." Sensing these words only further confirmed that it was time for him to relinquish all control and allow God to move. Andrew was one hundred percent on board with the decisions regarding my treatment. The difficult and agonizing period of waiting, researching, and deciding on a plan was over. It was officially, GO TIME.

12

The Silver Thread

"When I am afraid, I put my trust in you."
Psalm 56:3

Early that following week, we met with our physician assistant in the oncology department and told her that we had decided on our plan. She went over the first step of treatment which was beginning chemotherapy. She explained that I would be given a "chemo cocktail" called TC. This was a combination of two drugs called Docetaxel (Taxotere) and Cyclophosphamide (Cytoxan), and this snazzy little combo would be administered through a vein four to six times, once every 21 days. After the fourth cycle, my progress would be assessed by doing another breast MRI to determine if an additional two cycles of chemotherapy were recommended.

The goal was to shrink the tumor and potentially kill any other floater cancer cells with the chemo. Because of the type of cancer that I had, and its aggressive nature, going after it with both barrels blazing was important. Also, having the chemo first would, hopefully, make the upcoming surgery a bit easier in terms of getting all of the cancer removed. Personally, I wanted to do the chemo first because I was mentally and physically at a place where I was ready to fight. I knew this was going to be the hardest part for me and I wanted to take it on while I had some spunk. I also felt like the surgery would be a bit of a "butterfly moment" for me. After going through the trenches of chemo, I wanted the surgery to feel like a finishing touch. I wanted to feel new and put back together in some way, and in my mind, this is what made the most sense.

So there I was, ready to really begin my fight and I took a minute to reflect on the past three and a half weeks, that felt like years. The rollercoaster of emotions and the realization that I had to completely surrender myself to God, brought me into a mindset that I had never experienced before. I remember trying to explain this to a friend using an image that kept coming to my mind at the time. I kept seeing a cloudy, stormy, sometimes sunny landscape that represented my life. Some days were bright and beautiful, and others were downright tumultuous. But within that landscape was a thin silver thread that was constant, unwavering and strong. That thread was the Lord, and it was His peace that I was holding onto. It was the one thing that wasn't changing throughout the ever-changing scenery of each day, and it was the one thing that kept me going and looking forward with hope. Some may say that "every cloud has a silver lining," but I like to say that mine has a silver thread, and I was holding on for dear life.

Isaiah 12:2. "*Surely God is my salvation; I will trust and not be afraid. The LORD, the LORD, is my strength and my song; he has become my salvation.*"

13

Jamie's Top 10

Top 10 Realizations Now That I'm About to Lose My Hair in a Few Weeks

Drum roll, please....

10. It will now take my husband longer to do his hair in the morning than me!

9. When applying makeup, and specifically foundation on my face for those romantic evenings out, where do I stop?

8. I won't have to shave my legs all summer! SWEEETTT!

7. I'll finally be able to channel my inner "G.I. Jamie" and flex my guns and bark orders around the house and get away with it. Oh, yeah.

6. I will be able to try out that cute Audrey Hepburn pixie cut, once it starts growing back, that I've always secretly wanted to try, but was too chicken to.

5. I won't have to worry about that stray hair that annoyingly, and constantly, brushes your cheek, but you can NEVER find. Come on ladies, you know what I mean.

Top 10 Realizations Now That I'm About to Lose My Hair in a Few Weeks

4. I will need to renew my expiring passport pronto, or I'll be looking at my bald head for the next ten years!

3. If I do any volunteering in the cafeteria at my daughters' school, I won't have to wear a hairnet. BONUS.

2. O.M.G....My already "ginormous" forehead is going to be NEVER ENDING.

1. My girls will hopefully learn that true beauty is not about your outward appearance, but instead about your heart.

14

It's Chemo Day

"You armed me with strength for battle; you humbled my adversaries before me."
Psalm 18:39

Game on. The first day of being able to fight back against this monster was finally here. It was chemo day. I woke up feeling a little anxious, and I wasn't sure if it was the pre-chemo steroids I was on or my nerves. I was kind of hoping the steroids would send me into a roid-rage frenzy that would result in me spring cleaning my house and getting all of the laundry done and folded in record speed, but that didn't quite happen. Oh well, a girl could dream.

I got up early and was searching for some comfort, so I opened my *Jesus Calling* devotional again. The entry for that exact day began with: "Do not be afraid, for I am with you." I prayed and asked God to continue to give me peace. Then I grabbed my bag I packed the night before with all of the essentials I thought I might need for the day and off we went.

The first order of business was getting my port-a-cath put in. A port is a surgically inserted device that allows access to a central vein and would be the means by which I would receive my chemo infusions. The night before I was texting my friend, who was one step ahead of me in her chemo treatments, to ask her a few questions about this procedure. One of my questions for her was what type of shirt I should wear to the hospital. I wanted to wear something that was comfortable, but also convenient for accessing the port which would be placed just below my collar bone. After a quick text exchange and some good information transfer in terms of fashion choice, I started to laugh at the absurdity of it all. What in the world was happening? How can I be going through this right now? I should be texting my friend to ask her what cute shoes go with my outfit, not what sweater would best accessorize my port!

I was prepped for the port placement procedure and met the physician who would be doing it for me. When he walked into the room, I had to smile because he was wearing a surgical cap with the black and yellow University of Iowa logo on it. My alma mater! What are the chances that a fellow Iowa Hawkeye would be kicking off this show for me this morning? It definitely brought a smile to my face, and I may have tried to sing, or I should say, slur the fight song while the Versed sedative the nurses had given me was beginning to take over.

After a successful procedure, I was transported by wheelchair to the infusion services, and it was time for my chemo cocktail. The infusion nurses hooked up my IV with a full bag of Benadryl. The Benadryl is given to prevent a possible allergic reaction to the hard stuff, and the combination of the sedatives from the first procedure with the Benadryl was making me officially loopy.

I closed my eyes and was able to rest a bit while each drug was administered. Between rest breaks, I periodically dug in my bag and pulled out things to do while I waited. I read a Glamour magazine, because who doesn't want to feel glamorous while pumping poison through their body? Then I sniffed my little bottle of lavender essential oil because it was relaxing and helped me pretend that I was in a spa somewhere getting pampered instead of hooked up to an IV pole. I snacked on sprouted pumpkin seeds and guzzled water like it was going out of style. Lastly, I dug out a thick envelope that one of my Life Group friends gave me. It was three typed pages of Bible verses about healing. I read and reread all of them and tried to let them soak into my heart. I wanted to go into this fight armed with the best weapon I knew. God's Word.

Over the next few days, I continued to receive some beautiful encouragement from multiple people. One particular person sent me a card and included Isaiah 61:3. It said Jesus came to, *"provide for those who grieve in Zion—to bestow on them a crown of beauty instead of ashes, the oil of joy instead of mourning, and a garment of praise instead of a spirit of despair. They will be called oaks of righteousness, a planting of the Lord for the display of his splendor."* Four days later, another friend on the other side of the country, sent me a message with the exact same verse. In my mind, it was another confirmation that God was comforting me, hadn't left me, and was continuing to spur me on.

15

Why Me?

"I consider that our present sufferings are not worth comparing with the glory that will be revealed in us."
Romans 8:18

The first cycle of chemo was definitely a one-two punch. The initial side effects felt enhanced because I was also getting over the sedatives from the port placement procedure, and it was the first time my body had been introduced to its new pharmaceutical best friend. It pretty much felt like throwing a bomb into a barn to kill the mouse in the corner. The bomb is probably going to kill the mouse and maybe take out a couple more hiding under the hay bales, but the barn is going to take quite a beating, too. I ended up sleeping for the rest of the afternoon after coming home from receiving the first treatment.

The initial week came with a variety of side effects. The first day after my treatment my whole body felt shaky, and I was very dizzy. I also had some slight nausea that I did my best to combat with small meals, protein-packed smoothies, and a constant stash of bananas and toast with almond butter next to my bed.

Over the next couple of days, my hips and knees began to ache, and it wasn't the type of ache you feel after a hard workout. It was a throbbing, stabbing pain that I had never experienced before. I felt like I had just aged about twenty years. I limped around gingerly as the deep bone pain permeated my whole lower half. It started at my back and then it made its way down to my knees. I tried to keep moving and did slow laps around my yard like a pony in a ring.

Then the headache and thick tongue feeling set in. I could almost feel my tongue and throat begin to swell as I'm sure my lymph nodes were saying, "What the heck is happening?" They were in full combat mode, and they were letting me know it. I had also read about the metal taste that patients often experience with chemo, and they were right. Even water had a strange taste, and my tongue felt like it had been burned by an extremely hot piece of pizza.

The following evening the heartburn set in. I'm not one to experience heartburn regularly, so my first thought was, "Call an ambulance! I'm having a heart attack!" But once I came to my senses and realized that no, I wasn't going into cardiac arrest and that the culprit was some chemo-induced acid reflux, I calmed down a bit and started drinking water with peppermint oil and popping Tums. The only position that I could find to sleep somewhat comfortably was sitting straight up and slightly bent forward. Well, that doesn't lend itself to a restful night for your partner, so I vacated our bedroom and went into the living room. I propped myself in a chair, on my knees, facing the back of the chair in an upright position, and rested my forehead on a pillow. I actually fell asleep around three in the morning and awoke to my daughter standing next to me in her jammies with a worried and confused look on her face. Thankfully, that was the end of the heartburn, but the rest of the side effects lasted a few more days.

My oncology physician assistant had warned me that I would experience fatigue, but I thought, "Fatigue? Really? I can do fatigue. I've been tired before, and I'm really good at naps! I'll just take a nap, and I'll feel great!" Yeah...well, that's not the kind of fatigue that she was referring to. This was a type of fatigue that I had never experienced and still have a hard time putting into words. All I wanted to do was sit on the couch ALL DAY and for this on-the-go girl that is not a normal activity for me. Taking a walk around the block was a major undertaking and often resulted in a big celebration and a peanut butter, banana, protein powder smoothie reward. So, I learned to listen to my body, and let it rest as much as possible while still trying to keep moving. There were definitely days when I would get a little burst of energy and would feel slightly more like myself, and often times those were the days that I would overdo it and push my body a little too hard. It became a game of trial and error as I figured out what was too much, and what I could feasibly handle each day.

After going through the first six days of experiencing what it was like to have this powerful medication going to town on my insides, I was beginning to realize this wasn't going to be a walk in the park. This was going to be hard. The only way to sum up it up is to say that it felt a little bit like having the worst flu you've ever had and a bad hangover all at the same time. Unless someone has experienced chemotherapy for themselves, there is no way to fully comprehend what this treatment is like.

For those of you who have traveled this road, I applaud you and empathize. This was by far the hardest physical trial I had ever faced, and although I wasn't trying to invite myself to my own pity party, it was simply a fact. THIS WAS HARD! It was taking me to a place of complete physical and emotional brokenness and surrender. I had many moments when I questioned if this would ever end, and then somewhere in that darkness, a glimmer of normalcy would shine when I would actually entertain the thought of washing a dish or two. Most days that only lasted a second, mind you.

I asked myself many times, during those first few days, "Why? Why is this happening to me? Why do I have to face this trial? What did I do to deserve this? Why must my children watch me suffer? Why? Why do bad things happen to good people?" Now, I am not claiming to be any more "good" than anyone else. In fact, I'm quite flawed, broken, goofy and a work in process just like the next person. However, I'd like to think I don't have serial killer tendencies, I'm kind to animals, and I am that girl who will go all the way back to the Target cashier from the parking lot once I realize that small pack of gum that slipped through my cart at checkout, didn't get rung up. So again, why did I win the "your life is going to pretty much be crap for a while" lottery?

Well, it's actually very simple. We live in a fallen world. We live in a world that is not our home and on this earth, we will experience pain. It doesn't matter who we are or what we've done or not done with our life, we will experience trouble. John 16:33 says, "*I have told you these things, so that in me you may have peace. In this world, you will have trouble. But take heart! I have overcome the world.*" It doesn't say, your life will always be butterflies and rainbows and there will be an endless sale happening at Nordstroms! No, it says, you WILL have trouble. But you have to remember the last and best part of that verse. The promise that God wins. You win.

I believe that God has the power to prevent and cure disease and can choose to do that at any moment. However, I also believe that we will experience pain and suffering on this earth, and in my situation, He was allowing this to happen to me. I don't know why He chooses to do this, and by what grounds He makes that decision, but I do know that He will use every situation for good and as an opportunity for Him to be glorified.

This was going to be a time in my life when I was going to have to walk a difficult path, but it was my job to approach it with an attitude of thankfulness. Now please understand, I was not THANKFUL that I was dealing with cancer. I was not HAPPY about it one bit, and did I kick and scream and cry like a baby sometimes? ABSOLUTELY. But during these early days, I was learning to be grateful knowing a merciful God would never leave my side, and He would see me through to victory. I was learning to be grateful that He was giving me an opportunity to trust Him more, to see His incredible and constant love poured out on me each and every day, and then maybe I would be given the opportunity to use this experience to help someone else in the future.

I also started to choose to see the good this could produce in my family. My children were learning about a very real-life struggle and hopefully gathering tools about how to deal with trouble within a safe environment while they are young. I could have had the attitude that this was going to be an inconvenience on their perfect little lives, or I could choose to allow this to make them stronger and more equipped for what they will encounter as they grow. I could also choose to take this opportunity to teach them about compassion, fortitude, faith, trust, and chipping in when the chips are down. We all have a choice when it comes to how we view tough times in our life. I wasn't choosing to like it, but I did choose to accept and embrace it.

I knew I would have to remind myself of this all over again when it was time to put the gloves back on and jump in the ring for round two of chemo because having this mindset is hard work. It's not a flippant, happy-go-lucky attitude you just adopt. It takes daily prayer, internal wrestling, and literally throwing your hands up to the heavens and saying, "HELP!" Even in those moments when I struggled to wrap my head around everything that was happening, I decided to allow myself to be okay with not having all the answers and to find peace with that. So, my question became NOT, "Why me?" But instead...."Why not me?"

16

Fighting Mad

"The Lord is close to the brokenhearted and saves those who are crushed in spirit."
Psalm 34:1

It was a little over a week since my treatment, and I was feeling discouraged because my lab tests were showing that my white blood cell count was very low, which is typical for patients undergoing chemo. The tumor wasn't showing any signs of shrinking yet either, which didn't exactly help to lift my mood. I knew that it was still very early in my treatments, but I was desperately wanting to see some type of improvement. The good news was that the tumor wasn't growing, so I was happy about that.

One of the risks of an extremely low white blood cell count is that you are much more susceptible to getting an infection. Often times doctors can't even determine the source of the infection, but if it happens, it needs to be treated right away. We were given very specific instructions that if I began running a fever of 100.4 degrees or higher, I needed to call the hospital and most likely come in immediately.

Well, this overachiever did just that. During dinner one evening I started feeling chilled. I had actually begun feeling these chills earlier in the day but brushed them off as typical chemo side-effects. I had also avoided taking my temperature earlier because I really didn't want to end up in the hospital, and to avoid that destination, I kept telling myself that "no news is good news." Yeah, I know. Dumb. The "ignorance is bliss" approach wasn't working so well.

I excused myself from the table and went upstairs to lie down. I crawled under the covers to combat the chill in my bones, but at the same time, could feel my body temperature rising and sweat beginning to form on my brow. I knew what I needed to do, so I reached for the thermometer sitting beside my bed. It told me exactly what I knew it would. I had a fever of 102.4 degrees. Great. We made that dreaded phone call to the oncology doctor on call and drove into Urgent Care.

I was admitted to the hospital and given strong antibiotics to fight the infection. The medical staff placed me in a special room where I was slightly sequestered to protect me from further exposure to other germs because my immune system was toast. I spent two and a half days eating delicious hospital, gluten-free macaroni and cheese that seriously was amazing, and being still before God.

I didn't realize how much I actually needed that time to myself until it was forced upon me. I was feeling so emotionally heavy and beaten up. I needed some time to process everything that was happening and the feelings that came along with that. I was beginning to see the reality of how I wasn't going to be able to do the things I used to do, like taking my girls to the pool or cooking meals for my family. Those realizations were taking quite a toll. I felt completely helpless as I was forced to be still, laying in a hospital bed listening to the humming sound of the IV pump next to my head as it administered my antibiotics.

It was during this time that I began really crying out to God, and they weren't "pretty prayers." They were raw, angry, and honest prayers. I let out all of my frustration, all of my fear, and I unleashed on Him. I was completely overwhelmed and feeling incredibly alone. I feared for my life and for the physical battle that was raging inside of me at that very moment. I honestly wasn't sure who was going to come out as the victor, me or the cancer. As I laid on that hospital bed, tears rolled down the side of my face and soaked the stiff pillowcase. With the limited energy that I had left, I put it all on the table. God became my punching bag, and I let Him have it. I had nothing to lose, and I wanted answers. It was only the beginning of my fight with this nasty disease, but I was already sick of being sick. As I fought with God I could feel myself beginning to surrender both emotionally and physically. I knew I had to release all of my anger and fears to Him and as I did that, a weight began to lift slowly.

During that time, my phone buzzed, and a message popped up from a friend. It was the verse Isaiah 43:3. *"Fear not, for I have redeemed you; I have called you by name, you are mine. When you pass through the waters, I will be with you; and through the rivers, they shall not overwhelm you; when you walk through the fire you shall not be burned, and the flame shall not consume you. For I am the Lord your God, the Holy One of Israel, your Savior."*

I had to read and reread the message a few times because it touched a very deep and hurting place in my heart. It was exactly what I needed to hear at that very moment, and once again, God gave me that gentle touch and reassurance that I was crying out for desperately. I closed my eyes and truly rested for the first time in many days.

Over the next 48 hours, my counts slowly began to rise to a place where the doctors felt it was safe for me to go back home. Because of the hurried nature in which I ended up in the hospital, I didn't have a bag packed with all of my comfort essentials. Thankfully, my sweet husband brought in the basics like a toothbrush and some clean clothes to get me through those few days. Toward the end of my stay, I began to notice that my scalp was beginning to hurt as though I had a ponytail in for way too long. It felt like a dull ache all over my head, and I started to come to the realization of what was about to happen. It was probably time to start having some parting words with my hair, and I wasn't sure I was ready.

17

Hair Today, Gone Tomorrow

"I praise you because I am fearfully and wonderfully made; your works are wonderful,
I know that full well."
Psalm 139:14

I had known this day was coming for a while and it was finally here. I don't think you can truly be ready for this step of the process, even though I felt God preparing me for it for quite some time. I had asked a friend, who was also my hairdresser if she wouldn't mind being on call for me when it was time to take this step, and she graciously agreed. It was time for my hair to go, and I was calling in the professionals. Due to my time in the hospital with the absence of a hairbrush and many hours laying against the pillow, my hair had formed a large dreadlock on the back of my head. It was about the size of a grapefruit, and honestly, I was afraid to try to brush it out for fear of it all falling out in my hand. I was starting to see hairs beginning to loosen and come out easily, so I made the decision to be proactive and get ahead of the inevitable.

I contacted my friend right away, and she came to my home, armed with her cape, clippers, and her hundred-watt smile. I was worried about my daughters being afraid of seeing their mommy get her hair taken down to a buzz cut, so I decided to make it an upbeat moment and to include them in every step of it. It was a sunny spring day, so my husband and I set up a makeshift salon on the patio. We cranked up the volume on the outdoor speakers and piped in some happy reggae tunes. There's no better buzzing music than Bob Marley!

We put a towel around my shoulders while my friend got out her clippers. She turned them on, and the sound and vibration began to buzz in my ear. I could feel my stomach do a little flip, and I realized I was nervous. I was a little scared about this big step and how it would finally mark me as a cancer patient. It would be what would make this all incredibly real and visible, not only for myself and my family but for others around me. I wouldn't be able to hide the fact that I had cancer or pretend it away. But I knew I wanted to be strong for my girls and that this wasn't the time to let them know what I was feeling. So as the cold guard of the clippers touched the back of my neck, I took a deep breath, closed my eyes, and then looked up at my daughters, and smiled.

She started on the dreadlock, and slowly it began to loosen from the back of my head. The girls had a frisbee they had been playing with earlier, and they started to help by putting the chunks of hair that were falling off of my scalp into the frisbee. After they had seen a few good swipes, we asked them if they would like to give it a try. They both agreed, and with my friend's help, they each took turns shaving my head.

Lauren, my oldest, jumped at the opportunity and was very focused and eager as she did her job. Katherine was a little more timid, and I could tell she had some trepidation. She cut a little bit and then quickly resumed her responsibility of gathering the hair as it fell. Andrew even got in on the fun and did a few swipes himself. I can't imagine this was something he ever thought he would be doing someday with his wife!

Standing to the side were my parents helping, taking pictures, and just being an amazing support system for all of us. Along with Andrew and the girls, they were dressed in matching "TEAM JAMIE" t-shirts cheering me on. They made a point to stay positive and upbeat for my daughters, too, and I could tell that having them there in full support was helping the girls feel more at ease.

Once it was all done, my mom handed me a mirror, and I took a look at myself for the first time. My long hair was gone, and I saw a wide-eyed face with a quarter inch crew cut looking back at me. I felt lighter for some reason and grateful for both the physical weight of the hair being gone and for the emotional weight that was lifted, too. I had been anticipating this moment for quite some time, and to have finally crossed this milestone, was freeing. However, a sadness began to come over me as I grieved the loss of my normal, but I also knew that this was one step closer to getting to my finish line. I looked over at my mom, and for the first time that day, she started to cry. I immediately said, "Oh no, don't you start crying. You'll get me started, too!" But, she said, "No, I'm not crying because I'm sad. I'm crying because you're beautiful."

I had never imagined myself without hair, or what it would be like to wake up in the morning and look at myself in the mirror with no hair, eyebrows or eyelashes. And honestly, it was hard to come to grips with it. You may be thinking, seriously, it's just hair. And I completely agree, it is JUST hair. I had those days when I thought, "I will totally rock this!" as I scoured YouTube for videos of how to tie a turban and spent ridiculous amounts of money buying fun earrings online. But then I had that day when all I could do was sob uncontrollably in the shower while holding clumps of hair in my hands. It's still hard. I'm still a woman who wants to feel beautiful. When you are faced with this kind of reality, it forces you to dig deep within yourself and pull out things that you never realized needed to be dealt with before. When I allowed myself to do a little soul excavating, what I discovered was.... pride.

I realized that there was a small piece of myself that was pretty proud of the fact that I looked relatively decent for my age, could still get those, "O.M.G. you haven't changed since high school!" comments, and get carded once in a while in the grocery store. Okay, so maybe THAT hasn't happened recently, but a girl can dream! I found that at times I was putting more importance on my physical appearance than I should. Ladies, you know we all dress for each other, not for our men. Heck, our wonderful guys don't even notice when we color our hair! Seriously....they don't. Now, don't get me wrong, this girl loves everything visually beautiful and "fashiony," and that will never change, but I felt God was shining a soft beam of light on an area of my life that needed some attention.

I think it is very easy to become prideful. We are all so blessed! Many of us can say we have good jobs, intelligent minds, fabulous eyebrows, fantastic kids, or amazing talents, and there is nothing wrong with any of those things. But oftentimes, one or more of those possessions or attributes can be tainted with a slightly unhealthy dose of pride. Pride gets in the way of our ability to truly put other people and their needs first. It focuses too much attention inward instead of outward. Being completely humbled by this experience was showing me how all that stuff doesn't matter. It can all be gone in an instant, and when that happens, what are we left with?

By no means, do I believe that me losing my hair, or having cancer for that matter, was some type of punishment or "Godly smackdown" intended to penalize me for anything I have done or any character flaw I may have. However, I do believe God will use situations in our life to gently redirect our thinking or push us back on the road if we are floundering a bit in the ditch. Proverbs 31:30 says, "*Charm is deceptive, and beauty is fleeting; but a woman who fears the Lord will be praised.*" This is a good reminder that so much in this world is fleeting, and when my time here is done, I want to walk into heaven being praised for my fear in the Lord, and only that.

Hair grows back. (Preferably extremely thick, with no grays, and streaked with honey highlights please!) Eyelashes grow back, and so do eyebrows. But what I want to grow is a truer sense of the person God intended me to be. A person that knows how much He loves me no matter what I look like, and a person that can stay humbly focused on what really matters in life. So, I made the decision that I would take this next "punch in the face" step of shaving my head, with a stiff upper lip. With a new softness in my heart, I knew I was being molded into a more effective and empathetic person every day. With that comes great possibilities, and even better Halloween costume ideas.

18

Round Two

"But as for you, be strong and do not give up, for your work will be rewarded."
2 Chronicles 15:7

Here we go again! It was time to get my game face back on and jump into the ring for round two. I have to say, my fighting spirit wasn't quite as strong as it was going into my round one, primarily because I now knew what I was getting into. That first treatment cycle is shrouded with a bit of naivety which, I think, is a blessing. However, once you know what's coming with the subsequent cycles, you find that little spring in your step isn't quite as present as before. But at the same time, there is a familiarity with the process that is strangely comforting. Now, I knew approximately which days were going to be the toughest, what side effects might come and when, and I was slowly finding a rhythm in terms of my "post-chemo infusion routine."

I also got a fun little gadget this time to help with my predisposition for ending up with little to no white blood cells after treatment. It was an on-body injector that is intended to help boost white blood cell growth.

It's a little pack that sticks to your arm and injects a medication 27 hours after treatment. The fun part was that it blinked a green light every ten seconds which made it easy for my husband to track me when I got up in the middle of the night to use the bathroom. I also think my auntie cool factor went up in my nephew's eyes because I was now a female version of Buzz Lightyear.

The week before this second round was a good week and I actually had a few days of feeling relatively normal. I made it out to Target (whoa!) and even had a couple of quick lunch dates. It was wonderful getting out again and enjoying things I did "BC" (before cancer), but I noticed that it was still hard. I wasn't prepared for the strange looks from people that didn't know me, and the spontaneous waterworks when someone would ask me how I was doing. I found I could only be out in public for a few hours before I needed to go home, crawl under my sheets and hide for the rest of the day.

I knew it would get better as time went on, but those first few days of ripping off the Band-Aid of my new normal was tough. I also had to get used to the fact that my fun new haircut wasn't so cute anymore. My hair continued to fall out more and more each day, leaving a heavy dusting on my pillow every morning and on the collars of my shirts. It seemed to come out faster around my upper temples, and I began resembling an older man struggling with male pattern baldness. Yeah. It's kind of hard to prepare for that one. But again, it's all a process, and I adapted and grew with it daily.

This particular stage was also giving me a brief insight into the lives of people living with disabilities or physical deformities, and the struggles they face every day. By no means do I compare this temporary season of what I was going through to someone who lives with a permanent physical or cosmetic disability. However, I definitely experienced slight moments of what looking different compared to social norms is like. Those strange stares from the little kids at the grocery store or the double takes from people passing on the street were growing my empathy and love for those people who deal with feeling shockingly different every day of their lives.

I believe times like these that give us the ability to walk in someone else's shoes, even for a short time, are priceless. And when we're given the opportunity to step into that world and be enlightened, it's our responsibility to never forget it. As I continued down this path of being completely humbled, I felt God reminding me of 1 Samuel 16:7, "*...For the Lord sees not as man sees: man looks on the outward appearance, but the Lord looks on the heart.*" Again, it was a subtle reminder that I didn't need to be concerned about what people thought of how I looked, but that I needed to be more focused on my heart.

19

Holding My Hands Up

"Come to me, all you who are weary and burdened, and I will give you rest."
Matthew 11:28

One of the other struggles I had at this particular stage in the game, was that I was tired. SO tired. That initial emotional drain of coming up with the plan was over, but now it was the physical drain of executing the plan that was taking its toll. In the beginning, I was pressing into God so much and relying on Him for comfort and strength daily, but as time went on, I found myself becoming weary of even doing that. I knew I needed to remain close to Him, but my mental strength was taking a hit, too, and I was becoming overcome with my own version of "God guilt."

I felt guilty that I wasn't praying more and reading my Bible more, but I just couldn't do it, and for a perfectionist minded girl, it was eating me alive. Because I was in this rock-bottom place and the only hope I had was the Lord, I found myself believing the lie that I had to exert some supernatural effort to press that much harder into God. All the time. I was beginning to believe that I needed to tick off the boxes on that religious to-do list "For People Whose Lives Depend on It" and log enough hours on my knees to make it count. But my will and my foggy brain were having nothing of that. I started feeling like a failure and that my faith was weak. I often chastised myself for drifting away on those days when I knew I should pray, but just didn't want to. The only energy I felt I had left was going straight to basic functioning, and I honestly didn't have any reserves left in the tank.

I wrestled with this feeling quite a bit, but then I started to see a pattern developing. On those days when I was really beating myself up and feeling completely unmotivated to pray, I would get a message or a call from a friend telling me they were praying for me. Maybe it was the chemo brain. Yes, that's a real thing, but it took a few times of this happening for me to understand what God was trying to teach me. He doesn't ask us to fight our battles all by ourselves all of the time. In fact, He purposely brings in people around us to lift up our hands when we're too tired to do it ourselves.

As I explored this idea more, I began meditating on a beautiful example of this in Exodus chapter 17 when Moses is leading the Israelites through the desert to the promised land and are attacked by a hostile army of Amalekites. Moses orders Joshua to fight the Amalekites and then goes to the top of a hill with his brother, Aaron, and friend, Hur. Moses stands on that hill and begins to hold up his hands. Whenever he had his hands up, the Israelites were winning the battle, but whenever he lowered his hands, they would begin to lose. After doing this for what was probably quite a while, Moses got incredibly tired, so his faithful crew brought in a stone for him to sit on. Now, this is the best part. Aaron and Hur take their places on either side of him, and each takes one of his hands in theirs. They begin to hold up his hands and continued to hold them steady until sunset. Because of their help, Joshua was able to win the battle against the Amalekites and save the Israelite people.

Even Moses, who was a total Bible rockstar, got tired. He knew he had a part to play in this battle and he was determined to follow through, but he was unable to physically do it on his own. It took his friends and family to come beside him and hold up his hands. So many times, I wanted to be strong and fight this fight all by myself, but I didn't have the physical or emotional strength to do it. So, true to God's character, He brought people around me to lift up my hands, and I knew I needed to give myself some grace and allow them to do just that. It's often hard for me to ask for help or to even receive it, but if Moses needed a little hand-holding, then, I, for sure, could accept some for myself.

But he said to me, "My grace is sufficient for you, for my power is made perfect in weakness." Therefore, I will boast all the more gladly about my weaknesses, so that Christ's power may rest on me. —2 Corinthians 12:9

20

Be Still

"The Lord will fight for you; you need only to be still."
Exodus 14:14

The days continued to slowly tick by as I worked to manage and function while riding the familiar rollercoaster, I lovingly called the "Chemo Train." I was definitely the typical rider, both throwing my hands up and laughing on good days, and then gripping the safety bar for dear life and screaming my lungs out on the awful days. I had checked round two off my list and settled into the reality that after two comes…. three. So, when that day came, I wrapped up my turban, put on some fancy earrings and made my way to the hospital. You ask, "Who wears fancy earrings to chemo infusions?" Well, this chick does. I decided early on that I would not let cancer define me or change who I am or what I love. If I was going to have toxic chemicals pumped through my body in a sterile, bland environment, I was going to do it with some pizzazz!

This round didn't disappoint with the side effects and even blessed me with a couple of new ones, like hot flashes. I was told that chemo can put you into early menopause and, boy, they weren't kidding! It felt as though someone had just lit an internal combustion engine inside my body that would kick into high gear every few hours.

One morning, when we were getting ready for church, I put on a turtleneck sweater because it was still a little chilly early in the day. All of a sudden, I could feel my heart do the telltale flutter, and my engine started overheating. My face flushed and the only thing I knew to do at that moment was to go outside where it was cold. I took off like a flash toward the back door and left my husband standing in the kitchen, holding his cereal bowl with a look of utter confusion on his face. I opened the door, stood on the stoop and spread my arms out like a bird to help aid with the cooling. My husband's eyes preceded to get wide, and he said, "Oh my gosh, you're smoking!" Now, of course, I thought he was commenting on my gorgeous bald-headed looks, but no. I was actually smoking. Steam was rising off of both my body and my head, and it looked like I was on fire. We broke into hysterics, and I think for the first time he had a new appreciation for what I was dealing with, and he agreed that menopause was not for sissies!

I learned to manage my new symptoms but still found myself struggling with all that came with trying to recover from each round. But, as I clawed my way out of the dark pit of those post-treatment weeks, I took some time to look back on the recurring lesson I felt God had been teaching me and it was to BE STILL. Okay, seriously, I had a "What you talkin' bout Willis?" moment when He hit me upside the head on that one. Yep, I'm dating myself with the "Different Strokes" reference so thank you to all of you who can relate. Oh, and yes, I got hit on by Gary Coleman when I lived in Los Angeles years ago. Couldn't have been Brad Pitt, nope, Gary Coleman. Different story for a different day.

As you have probably gathered, I like to be moving and doing, and getting stuff DONE! The thought of being still just isn't in my wheelhouse. But when your life comes to a screeching halt due to an illness or a tragedy, you learn that, shockingly, life continues to happen around you and without your help. I am so guilty of getting caught up in the rat race and the call of the to-do list, so this was a tough nut for me to crack. I like checking things off lists, a... lot. I will even write ridiculous things on my list just so I can cross them off. Brush teeth, CHECK! Make a list of my lists CHECK! The thought of being still was a new one for me.

Chemo is the equivalent of running at full speed into a brick wall. You guessed it. You are physically stopped cold. Especially during the rough days, I was forced to literally sit, and that was the extent of my movement. Thankfully, it was spring, and the warm weather allowed me the sheer joy of sitting outside and really absorbing God's creation. I started really noticing birds and the beauty of their song. I actually saw flowers and how perfect each petal was. I began closing my eyes and listening to the gurgling of our water fountain in our garden and soaking in the gentle breeze in my hair. By hair I mean in the singular sense. Yep, I still had a couple of stubborn ones that just wouldn't let go! Come on! Give it up already, you stragglers! You're making me feel like a bald baby bird!

I was finding that if we don't allow ourselves the grace to be still, we miss out on so much. We miss out on the chance to rejuvenate our bodies and our minds. We miss out on the countless little miracles that happen around us on a daily basis. We miss out on the opportunity to spend time with God and have Him speak to us and pour into our souls.

Psalm 46:10 says, *"Be still and know that I am God..."*. It's a direct command to stop running for a minute. Be still. I know that looks different for everyone and we all are created with specific paths for recharge, but for me, it became a routine of sitting, closing my eyes, putting away all technology, and praying. Carving out a specific time to do this, and not just on the fly when you're running out the door or sitting in the carpool line, is the key. In the past, I always found time for God throughout my day, but I never made the dedicated decision to be still each day. It's amazing what God will tell you when you are quiet enough to listen.

The pursuit of being still isn't a new concept for many of us. We are often reminded of this, and even more often it's in the two-dimensional context of simply not moving so fast in our daily lives. However, if you dive into Psalm 46 in its entirety, there is way more to it than that. It begins in verse one through three with *"God is our refuge and strength, an ever-present help in trouble. Therefore, we will not fear, though the earth give way and the mountains fall into the heart of the sea, though its waters roar and foam and the mountains quake with their surging."* This is so often where we are when we're in the thick of the fight. We feel as though we are being swallowed up by the roar of the sea and everything is falling down around us. But these verses show us that we don't need to fear the destruction that is beating down our door.

If you continue reading, verse seven goes on to reassure us of God's unwavering presence. *"The Lord Almighty is with us; the God of Jacob is our fortress."* Then God flexes his muscles and in verse nine begins showing us how He is fighting our battles for us. *"He makes wars cease to the ends of the earth. He breaks the bow and shatters the spear; he burns shields with fire."* Yes! That's what I'm talking about! God will do the heavy lifting for us! Only after He shows us how His mighty power will step in and do the hand to hand combat on our behalf does He command us to *"Be still, and know that I am God..."*

In the New American Standard version, the "be still" part is translated as, "cease striving." I'll say that again. Cease striving. To strive means to struggle or fight vigorously. We can actually take ourselves off the hook and stop struggling to fight our own battles. We have a God that delights in doing that for us. So, sit back and watch God go to the front lines for you, and if He has already fought one of your battles at some point in your life, then reflect and remind yourself of that regularly. Never forget it because He will do it again, and again, and again.

As I continued to recover from the latest treatment cycle, I made a vow to myself to daily try to be still. It is NOT easy, and I would be lying if I said I've got this thing down. It's a discipline, not just a decision. I knew I needed to start working on strengthening my "be still muscles" every day. I had to both physically be still in God's presence and also cease striving to fight my own battles.

But what a perfect season this was to start. The early days of summer were dawning, and typically this is supposed to be a time of year where we enjoy moments of rest and reflection. You're probably asking, "What is that?" No matter what "season" it is, ask yourself where you can find time to be still in your day. What is SO important that it comes before your well-being or your relationship with God? What battle do you need to stop trying to win all by yourself, and are you willing to give it over to God and allow Him to crush whatever opponent is pressing you?

Trust me, when you are faced with a life or death experience, your priorities change. Even fifteen minutes of quiet can be incredibly life-giving, and who doesn't need to have their hearts poured into? We all give so much of ourselves every day to people, jobs, and families. Allow yourself to be filled back up again, take off the boxing gloves and just...be still.

21

FOUR

"My flesh and my heart may fail, but God is the strength of my heart and my portion forever."
Psalm 73:26

At this point, I had completed chemotherapy cycle three and was slowly recovering from the latest assault on my system. A definite pattern had emerged with each cycle of chemo, and I could relatively predict which days I would feel the best and which days I would feel the worst. The first week or so after the infusion was always the toughest and then as time went on, I would progressively feel a little better and get some of my energy back just in time to have another infusion.

I was noticing, however, that as I progressed through these cycles, I wasn't snapping back as quickly or as fully. I could tell that my body was getting very weary, wasn't recovering as well, and I was beginning to feel like one of those inflatable punching bags for kids that looks like a column with a menacing wrestler face on it. It's a toy that has a weight strategically placed in a rocker style base that keeps it grounded and so it can pop back up when kicked or punched. It takes the hit but then rocks up to an upright position poised to take another beating. Well, each time I took a kick or punch, I lost a little air and didn't quite come back to center again, and after each round, I was continuing to recover a little less successfully.

I could really feel the physical strain that everything was taking on my body and I was starting to get scared. When we had originally decided on my treatment plan months earlier, my oncologist told me I could have anywhere from four to six chemo infusions total, but we wouldn't know that final number until I went in for my fourth cycle. As I progressed through the first two cycles, and into the third, I became more and more anxious about how many I would have to endure.

The physical toll that chemotherapy has on you, literally and figuratively, takes your breath away. I knew they were helping me in the long run, and I was trying my best to persevere until the end, but it was hard. I wasn't sure if I was going to be able to make it to cycle four let alone to a possible cycle six, and I wouldn't know which it would be until the morning of my fourth infusion. It was up to my oncologist to make the decision whether she felt that the chemo had done its job and the tumor had shrunk to an optimal size. Only then might I receive my get out of jail free card and be able to walk away after four cycles. If she wasn't satisfied with the results and felt the tumor needed a little more punishing, then I would be adding an additional two more cycles of the hard stuff. But even though I wasn't sure that my body or my mind could take the continued effects that the treatments were having on me, and I was losing faith that I could make it even one step further in this journey, I felt God calling me to simply trust in Him.

One night I was struggling to fall asleep, and the extreme fatigue was completely taking over. I was feeling awful. I know, that doesn't make any sense and you're probably thinking if you're so tired, then just sleep! No big deal! But this type of fatigue isn't just the kind that makes you want to close your eyes and drift off into a blissful dream world. It's the kind that keeps you awake at night because you can feel your joints aching, your temples buzzing, and your whole body fighting.

This was one of those specific nights, and I found myself in a very dark and desperate place. Psalms 23 began to materialize for me in complete technicolor at that precise moment. I felt like I was literally walking *"through the valley of the shadow of death."* As I closed my eyes and tried to breathe through the discomfort, I experienced something that even to this day is hard for me to describe. There was a moment when I could feel a distinct separation between my soul and my body. Yes, I get it. Thoughts of all of the good medically prescribed drugs that I was probably on are coming to mind, right? Well, that was definitely not the case. I wasn't taking any medications, so this was a real and very raw awareness of something happening inside of me.

It felt as though my body was a broken shell, actively trapping my spirit inside. It wasn't an out of body experience, but rather a dark and gritty moment where my mind and soul desperately wanted to break out of my physical prison, but couldn't. I could feel the life force that makes me who I am, fighting against the shell of my physical body, and there was a definite separation between the two. The former, my spirit, felt great and alive and vibrant, but the latter, my body, felt like a hard metal frame of a car that had its engine torn out. For the first time in my life, I was aware of these two very separate pieces of my being, and it scared me, and all I had left in my reserve tanks to fight were a few words that I began to repeat over and over in my mind. "I trust you, Jesus… I trust you, Jesus… I trust you, Jesus…" I said this over and over, silently crying until I was finally able to drift off to sleep.

So, after my third cycle, my daily plea, because you could hardly call it a prayer at this point, was that God would spare me from having to endure six treatments. Four was all I physically thought I could bear. Every day I would beg, reason and implore God to make four my magic number. Because of the anxiety and stress I was feeling at this point, we knew I needed a change of scenery. So, once I was feeling well enough to travel, Andrew and I drove back up north to my parents' lake home to get away and rest. Once again, we knew we needed to get close to nature and feel the peace of this wonderful place. The gentle wind in the pines and haunting loon calls in the evenings have soothed my heart so many times before, and this time was no exception.

When we first arrived, the girls catapulted out of the car and began unpacking and exploring as they always do. I slowly made my way to the couch to catch my breath and look out on the lake. Soon the two of them came barreling inside to tell me that they had made an exciting discovery! They took me out to our canoe which was sitting outside on the grass and sheltered inside its hull was a tiny treasure. A perfectly formed nest with four small untouched eggs was resting inside. I think it was the most beautiful nest I had ever seen. It was absolutely perfect in every way. Completely untouched and pristine. I remember feeling incredibly moved by the simplicity of it, and yet the complexity of the new life it represented. That night I laid in bed and thought, could it be? Could God be telling me it was going to be four treatments just like the four eggs in the nest? Is He going to answer my prayers? No, that was crazy. I was so desperate that I was REALLY grasping for straws now. I told myself, "Let it go, Jamie, it's a nest. That's all."

The next day, I felt well enough to ride into town with the family to explore the quaint streets and shops. The pine tree lined road that leaves our home and meets up with the highway is hugged on either side by ponds and bays full of wildlife and foliage. There is one particular pond we affectionately call "Turtle Pond" because for as long as I can remember, there has been a dead log in the center of the pond where turtles love to sun themselves in the summer. Over the years, the log has deteriorated, but someone who must also love our little turtle friends had built a small floating platform for them to continue their sunbathing.

The girls and I have a tradition of counting the turtles on the box each time we drive or walk by. The number of little sun worshipers can range from zero to 12 or more, depending on the day. As our car approached Turtle Pond, I thought, "I wonder if there will be FOUR turtles on the box today. Wouldn't that be cool!" I pretty much threw it out there as a test for God, or maybe myself, to see if I was really crazy or not. Honestly, I really didn't have much faith that there would be four, but the thought did cross my mind. So as our car approached, I asked my Dad to slow down a bit. I looked over and saw a little collection of turtles' backs glistening in the sun. I began to count. I counted again. Yep, one, two, three, four. OOkkaaayyyy….. I sat back in my seat and smiled.

At this point, I finally told Andrew about the theory that was beginning to form in my head. In the past, both Andrew and I have noticed that God likes to speak to both of us through nature. Psalm 19:1 says, *"The heavens declare the glory of God; the skies proclaim the work of his hands."* Andrew listened and encouraged me that maybe God was speaking to me and that I should continue to trust and believe in His promises. I still wasn't convinced though, but I secretly hoped he was right.

The following morning was the beginning of our last day in this little paradise. I asked Andrew if he would take me for a canoe ride because I love being on the water. Knowing I wouldn't have the strength to actually paddle, I sat in the front of the canoe with my bald head covered by a wide-brimmed straw hat. I did my best princess impression as my handsome prince paddled me around the lake. It was glorious.

He steered us toward a large island positioned ahead of us, and as we approached its shores, I noticed a female duck swimming ahead moving toward the island banks. I squinted through the sun bouncing off the water and noticed that the duck was not alone. It looked as though she had some ducklings dutifully following her, but it was hard to tell from our distance. I pointed her out to Andrew, and he said, "Let's go closer! I wonder how many ducklings she has!" I immediately said, "NO! I don't want to bother her!" But truthfully, I was curious, too. I had a feeling about how many we might see, and yet I didn't want to be disappointed if I was wrong.

Andrew kicked up the paddling pace, and we began closing the gap between us and the little family. As we got closer the ducklings began to separate, and we were able to count them more clearly. One…. two…. three….and…. oh my gosh……...four. I immediately burst into tears and was overcome with the most infusing blanket of peace I have ever felt. I knew, at that moment, I would only have four chemo treatments, and that is exactly the news I received a few days later from my doctor.

Four. Four treatments. As I sat on the crinkly paper of the exam table during that much-anticipated appointment with my oncologist and heard those words come out of her mouth, I said, "Thank you, Jesus." Then, I hung my head, and cried.

That we have a God who loves us so much that He would orchestrate His own creation to speak His love to us, continues to blow me away. He is faithful. His love never fails. He is bigger than any problem we may have, and He knows us so intimately that He will choose ways to communicate with us that touch us in the deepest places of our hearts. Job 12:7-10 says, *"But ask the animals, and they will teach you or the birds in the sky and they will tell you, or speak to the earth, and it will teach you, or let the fish in the sea inform you. Which of all these does not know that the hand of the Lord has done this? In his hand is the life of every creature and the breath of all mankind."*

As we allow ourselves to be open to the Holy Spirit and aware of the many ways He tries to communicate with us, we begin allowing the blessing of beautiful communication with our Creator into our lives. He will speak to us through multiple ways if we only ask Him for help and open our eyes and our hearts. I wasn't hearing the audible voice of God, but in this situation, I heard and saw His merciful promises through something that I love and that He created -- nature.

22

Tumor, Tumor Go Away

"Trust in the Lord with all your heart and lean not on your own understanding;
in all your ways submit to him, and he will make your paths straight."
Proverbs 3:5-6

That morning of my fourth and final chemo cycle, I wrapped my head in one of my favorite pastel colored scarves and put on a flashy pair of dangle earrings. I was going to go to this party in style! I won the infusion lottery that day and was given a private room with a window. The sun was streaming in adding its glory to the festive and celebratory mood that was already bubbling up from my family members and myself. Even though I wasn't looking forward to another series of side-effects, I was excited that this would be the last time I would have to look at those four hospital walls and sit in that plasticky infusion recliner.

Toward the end of my drip session, the lengthy act of receiving the chemotherapy drugs that is as about as exciting as watching paint dry, my door opened, and the entire nursing staff came into the room blowing bubbles, shaking noisemakers and singing a catchy song about my completion of chemotherapy. It was like being sung "Happy Birthday" at a Mexican restaurant, minus the sombrero, but WAY better! I was able to quickly record the moment on my phone although it wasn't the best quality because the IV bag of Benadryl had taken effect and I was totally three sheets to the wind. I ended up with a jumpy video of the nurse's feet and me giggling in the background. After the sweet and peppy serenade, I was handed a completion certificate to signify I had graduated from "chemo college" and sent home to recover for the last time.

From this point on, we all found quite a bit of joy in the "lasts". During the previous cycles, I kept a chart of my side effects so I would be able to effectively communicate them to my oncologist during checkups, and we numbered the days post-treatment for clarification. Typically, days three through seven were the worst, but now we referred to them as the "last day three" or the "last day six." Knowing this was the last time I would have to see a "day three" again, gave me just enough jet fuel to propel me to that finish line.

About two weeks later, I had another MRI. I hadn't had one since my diagnosis, and I was very anxious about this test. This was like getting my final grade on the big exam. I had done all of this work to get to this point and, darn it, I wanted it to be worth it.

I knew that the chemo was working because we could feel the tumor getting smaller and getting harder to find on self-examinations. But I don't like to do things halfway, and I wanted that nasty thing gone. Not just sort of gone; no, all the way gone. I prayed daily that God would take the tumor completely away and that the MRI results would show nothing. I reached out to all my prayer warrior friends with this one request, and I was believing with all of my heart that when the radiologist and surgeon looked at the images, they would find no cancer whatsoever. I was praying for a miracle and trusting God to deliver big time on this one.

So, when it was time to go in for my appointment to get my results from the test, I was edgy. I think my tendency to be a perfectionist was kicking into overdrive, too. I didn't want to fail. For some reason, I felt if there was still cancer showing on the MRI, that I hadn't done my job and that I was a failure. I know now, that was a lie that the enemy was using to try to discourage me and to shake my faith, but at the time it was my reality.

Andrew and I were escorted back to the exam room, and I rattled off my name and birthday to the nurse like I had done so many times before. The surgeon came into the room and sat at the desk next to our chairs. He pulled up my MRI on the computer and tilted the screen so we both could see it. My heart was pounding, and my eyes quickly searched the image for something, anything. I didn't even really know what I was looking at or looking for on the murky black and white image, but what I did see made my heart sink. A small blob of bright white contrast over the area of the tumor jumped out at me, and it felt as though all of the air had been let out of my chest.

The surgeon started with the good news which was that the tumor had indeed shrunk, but according to the MRI, there was still a small part of the tumor that looked like viable cancer. Ugh. C+. In my mind, the A+ grade I was hoping for just got knocked down to an average one. I felt defeated, angry, and exhausted. I thought for sure God was going to answer this request. He had been so faithful all along, and this would have been the cherry on the top of the sundae for me. Why God? Why couldn't it have been completely gone?

The surgeon reminded us that these were still very good results and the chemo had done its job of shrinking the tumor and making the upcoming surgery that much easier. I tried to put on my happy face, but I was still disappointed. When you're living with a disease in your body that has the potential to take you out all you want to do is take IT out.

It feels like an intruder that has broken into your home and has made themselves very comfortable on your living room couch. Not only are they taking up prime real estate in your house, but then they start eating everything out of your fridge and begin calling their nasty buddies to come over and walk away with all your valuable possessions. Meanwhile, all you can do is sit there and watch it all happen. If this were a true scenario, you would probably want to pick the guy up by his ear and heave him out the front door faster than you can say "Sayonara Bucko!" Well, that's what I wanted to do to this little intruder in my body, and I was mad that he was still sitting on my couch, eating my chips.

23

Phase Two

"...the Lord will watch over your coming and going both now and forevermore."
Psalm 121:8

I had just completed the first phase of "Operation Kick Cancer's Hind End," and now it was time to move onto phase two. Phase two was a double mastectomy with reconstruction, and I was so ready for this. In my mind, I always felt like this stage would be where I would start to see the light at the end of the tunnel. I had done my best "Little Engine That Could" impression chugging up the steep and treacherous mountains for months, and now I was nearing the summit where I could begin a slightly easier trek back down the mountain. It was much easier for me to wrap my brain around recovering from surgery than recovering from chemotherapy.

Being a dancer, I was used to injuries, and I had studied a pre-physical therapy major in college, so I was familiar with how the body worked and healed. So, the thought of recovering from surgery felt familiar and doable. I understood how swelling worked, and the importance of stretching and strengthening your muscles when the time was right during the recovery. I knew how to work on my range of motion and how the body heals itself after physical trauma. That is why I welcomed this stage with open arms compared to chemo. With chemo, there were too many unknowns for me, but surgery? I've got this.

But even with the excitement of knowing I was close to ticking this box off my treatment plan, I was still nervous. While I was wrestling with the fluttering butterflies in my stomach, I received a card from my aunt. On the front of the card, there was a painted image of an operating room and two surgeons focusing intently on performing a procedure on a patient. Standing next to one of the surgeons was the image of Jesus gazing at the patient and lightly guiding the surgeon's hand. The artist had painted beautiful lighting around Him, and His white robe was radiating with light. These are the words that my aunt wrote in the card:

Dear Jamie,

I love this visual of Jesus being present in the operating room, guarding the surgeon's every move. He WILL be there with you! Keep this picture in your head as you drift off to sleep. Let the name of Jesus be on your lips till you are no longer conscious. We have been, will be and continue to pray for you. We love you so much. Let God give you the peace and assurance of all that He is and all that is available through Him! There is nothing that can separate you from the love of God. Angels will surround you. They will be nudging each other with their wings to get the best spot to witness God's work through the doctors. But of course, Jesus will have the best seat in the house.

This imagery immediately gave me comfort, and I meditated on that picture in my mind for days. I felt peace knowing that Jesus would be in that operating room with me gently guiding the surgeon's hands and that, once again, He wouldn't leave my side.

As the day of surgery got closer, the reality that I was going to be losing my breasts started to sink in. There are many emotional ups and downs a woman experiences when they know they are going to have a mastectomy, and everyone deals with those emotions differently, but all are true and valid. It can be very difficult to think about losing a part of your body that makes you feel feminine and beautiful. I had someone tell me that I would essentially be a double amputee. For some reason, that really hit me. I had never thought about it that way before, and it was a little hard to hear. However, the desire to rid my body of something that could harm me far outweighed my grief of losing my breasts.

I reminded myself of 1 Peter 3: 3-4 that says, *"Your beauty should not come from outward adornment, such as elaborate hairstyles and the wearing of gold jewelry or fine clothes. Rather, it should be that of your inner self, the unfading beauty of a gentle and quiet spirit, which is of great worth in God's sight.* My "beauty" was fleeting quickly, but my outward appearance didn't matter. What did matter was doing what was going to keep me around on this earth longer to raise my children, be there for my family, and carry out the plan and purpose that God has for me. It's my heart that the Lord sees, and this body is temporary. Thankfully, with modern medical technology, I had the option to have breast reconstruction, and I decided that instead of being sad about losing my breasts, I was going to celebrate the fact that I would have a 2.0 version!

A couple of days before surgery, I had a date with my radiologist to get a small radioactive seed implanted near my tumor. The purpose of this seed was to help the surgeon precisely locate the tumor and then aid him in removing it completely. After the seed was implanted, I was given a wrist band with the international radiation symbol and sent home. I was told that the levels of radiation within the seed were extremely low, so it was safe to be around and hug my children. I couldn't help but think of Doc Brown from the *Back to the Future* movies, wearing his white radiation suit with the same symbol on the back. Maybe if I jumped in my car and sped off down the street at 88 miles per hour, I could go back to the future and skip this whole thing!

Knowing there was no chance of that, I packed my overnight bag, found an oversized denim dress at Target that buttoned all the way down the front, and a few days later I checked into the hospital to get prepped for surgery. I was taken back to the pre-op area and actually got a little excited when they put an IV in the top of my left hand. Up until now, any blood draws or anything that needed to be administered through an IV were done through the port in my chest. But the port, which bulged like an oversized round Lego stuck under my skin, was coming out! I couldn't be more excited about losing this piece of hardware that, for months, I had babied, protected, and strategically covered up as to not scare small children. Goodbye port, it's been nice knowing you! I also had to laugh when they put a surgical cap on me, considering I didn't have any hair. At this point, you find humor in just about anything.

The nurses started administering a drug to relax me, and the last thing I remember was my wonderful plastic surgeon talking about how he eats peanut butter and jelly sandwiches every day for lunch. His sweet bedside manner helped me drift off to la la land with a smile.

The procedure consisted of a double mastectomy where all of my breast tissue was removed from both breasts. Then a crescent-shaped piece of skin was also removed over the site of the tumor to safeguard against any potential skin involvement or reoccurrence in that area. I was left with an inch and a half scar where the piece of skin was taken and long sweeping scars under both breasts where the surgeon was able to remove the tissue. A lymph node dissection was also performed on my affected side, and the two sentinel lymph nodes were removed and tested while I was still in surgery for any evidence of cancer. The port was also removed, and then the baton was handed to the plastic surgeon.

While the surgeons tag-teamed in the operating room, and my parents and husband waited anxiously in the waiting room for over five hours, I took a nice, long nap. I had the easiest part all day! I don't even remember being rolled into the operating suite, and in what felt like a blink of an eye, I was waking up in recovery. As I opened my eyes, I saw the smiling face of a nurse hovering over me adjusting my pillows and saying to another nurse next to her, "Oh, I just want to take her home with me." Oh geez. What the heck did I say while I was under the influence of anesthesia? Who knows what crazy secrets I divulged to some absolute strangers? How embarrassing!

I made the choice to stay the night in the hospital even though I could have gone home that evening. For me, I felt more comfortable being under the care of a wonderful medical staff, and I also knew it would take some burden off of my husband and my parents. The only room available in the hospital was on the pediatric floor which was a treat. There's something very comforting about having woodland animals painted on the walls of your room and knowing that there are endless supplies of suckers on hand if I were to have a random craving.

My daughters came to visit me that next morning and walked in the room wearing t-shirts that said "My mom is my superhero," thanks to my thoughtful mother. I felt like they were my superheroes and had endured so much the past few months, so I was just as happy for them that we were all in this final stage of this long process.

I could see the initial trepidation on their faces when they came into my room, but once they saw me smiling and sitting up in the chair next to my bed, they relaxed a bit. Having been given the reassurance that mommy was fine, they proceeded to jump on my hospital bed and test out the tilting controls as only a six, and seven-and-a-half-year-old can do. This was all done much to the chagrin of the nurse on duty.

After I had successfully walked a few slow laps around the hospital floor with my husband, I was cleared to go home. This is where the full button dress from Target came in very handy again. I wasn't allowed to raise my arms above my head to pull a shirt on so being able to carefully slip my arms into my sleeves using a side motion was much easier. I had also been given a tip to get button-up pajamas, for this same reason, and loose sweat pants that don't require a ton of tugging to pull up for making using the restroom easier. I was going to need to baby my arms and pectoral muscles for a while. I guess I'd have to put my skinny jeans on the shelf for the time being. No pouring myself into those puppies anytime soon!

24

Hurry Up and Wait

"I can do all this through him who gives me strength."
Philippians 4:13

It was time to begin the next phase of recovery, and I was given the very strict instructions not to lift anything over ten pounds. My chest was wrapped with what looked like a medical tube top with a Velcro closure down the front, and I had two drains on either side of my ribcage. My homework each day was to empty the drains and clean the insertion sites. Thankfully, I had a fantastic home medical team which consisted of my mother who is a retired nurse, and my two daughters. The girls had been so involved in my journey up to this point, and there was no reason to stop now.

We asked them if they wanted to help with this process and they jumped at the opportunity. My mother did a wonderful job of teaching them the proper way to clean and change my dressings. After the first demonstration, they routinely gloved up and reported to their respective posts. Lauren cleaned the wounds, measured the drainage output with great accuracy and took her role very seriously. She did a beautiful job of recording each measurement and assisting my mother with the sterile dressings. Katherine's task was sitting on the bed, intently locking her eyes with mine, and guiding me through deep breathing exercises. She would hold my hand and say in her most calming yet dramatic yoga instructor voice, "Now mommy, breathe in….and breathe out…. breathe in….and out…. "

The drains were not very comfortable so, surprisingly, the deep breathing was very helpful and staring into those little faces of two sweet girls taking their jobs so seriously, was a great distraction. I found myself getting very cold during this process, so my two little caregivers, under the guidance of their teaching nurse, would wrap my head with blankets so I wouldn't shiver. No one told me how cold it is not having hair! I don't know how Mr. Clean can run around wearing that little, white t-shirt all the time!

The first-week post-surgery was devoted to getting physically stronger and looked fairly similar to the weeks after my chemo treatments, with a few exceptions. This time I couldn't lift anything, and I was required to keep my arms fairly still to decrease the pain and potential for additional swelling. However, I could move my forearms as much as I wanted to, so for any children out there having a dinosaur themed birthday party needing a T-Rex impersonator, I was their girl. I had completely mastered the "glue your arms to your sides, bend at the elbows, and only slightly move your hands" motion. It was quite a sight, but what was even more fun was watching my daughters put toothpaste on my toothbrush and button my pajama top each night. Oh, how the roles had changed!

I was excited about this stage of the game plan because it signaled the end, but what I wasn't prepared for was how frustrating it was to have another physical setback because of the surgery. When your name tag reads "Mrs. Couch Potato" for the past four months, and it typically reads "Mrs. Go Like Crazy and Get Stuff Done," it's hard to wrap your head around the fact that, just because the chemo is over, you can't jump back into the fast pace that you would prefer to right away. It was really hard to be still and wait for my body to heal.

One of the verses that I prayed over myself frequently during this time was Isaiah 40:31. *"But they who wait for the Lord shall renew their strength; they shall mount up with wings like eagles; they shall run and not be weary; they shall walk and not faint.*" For a while, I found myself focusing more on the last part of that verse which promises renewed strength and physical vitality. It wasn't until this time in my recovery that the "WAIT" part of that scripture really hit home. Patience has not been one of my strengths. But I see now how important it is to wait on God, still do your part, but wait on His perfect timing for all things in your life. Even if it's a strong body and a clean bill of health. Sometimes, things take time, and His timing is always better than our own.

While I waited and tried desperately not to overdo it each day, I began to look forward to outings with my family. I couldn't drive because I wasn't able to handle a steering wheel quite yet, so I got to play "Driving Miss Daisy" and was chauffeured by my husband and my parents quite frequently. Because of my physical restrictions, I couldn't buckle my seatbelt or open my car door myself, so this limitation led to some funny scenarios.

One, in particular, happened on a hot and sunny summer day. My mother and I were arriving home from a doctor's appointment. I had just had my last drain removed. We were celebrating this much-welcomed milestone and were in particularly good spirits because I was finally at a stage in my treatment and recovery, where I was feeling and acting a bit more like myself. My energy was slowly returning, and we were getting out of the house a little more, too.

We had stopped to grab a few groceries before heading home and continued to chat until we pulled into my driveway. My mother got out of the driver's seat, grabbed a couple of grocery sacks from the back, closed her car door, and went into the house to unload the bags. My daughters were there playing with a babysitter and, true to fashion, attacked their grandma with hugs and tugs into the other room to show her what they had been up to all afternoon.

A few minutes went by as I waited for her to come back outside and open my car door. I continued to wait in the passenger seat, buckled in, and unable to open the door myself. I was under strict doctor's orders not to do any pushing with my arms quite yet. I probably could have tried, but my parents' car has particularly heavy doors and, even before the surgery, those doors were difficult for me to open. I knew I needed to be a good, compliant patient, so waited in the car. I was sure she would emerge from the house to come and let me out of the car momentarily. Because if you know my mother, she is the most conscientious and thoughtful person, especially when it comes to her family.

But a few minutes ticked by, and a few more, and I was starting to get hot. Couple that with the chemo-induced, menopause hot flashes, and I was on fire! Just as I began mentally formulating my plan on how I was going to strategically lean enough to the left so I could reach the car horn to get her attention, the back door of the house flew open, and out she ran with a horrified look on her face. She sped around the front of the car and opened my door as a rush of cool air poured in. I looked at her and said, "You left the baby in the car!"

She was absolutely mortified that she had forgotten to help me out of the car, but we both laughed at the absurdity of the situation. It helped us realize how tired and weary we all were becoming with this journey, even for my caregivers. The glimpses of normalcy in my physical recovery were beginning to shine their light, and something about those slight reminders, takes you back to those good and easy days. It takes you back to a time before this freight train knocked, both you and your loved ones, off your tracks, and occasionally you find yourself forgetting that things aren't quite normal yet.

The sheer exhaustion of always being "on" and trying to be on top of every situation was taking a toll on all of my family members, and my sweet mother was not immune to this reality either. Even the most caring and capable people who would do anything for their loved ones have moments when they're human. What this situation did for us was to remind us that it's okay to not always be "on". We're all human. And when you're tired and feeling a little brain dead, whether you're the one strapped in the passenger seat or the one charged with opening the car door, it's important to always keep your sense of humor. A good laugh is always the best medicine.

25

Did I Hear That Right?

"For the Lord your God is the one who goes with you to fight for you against your enemies to give you victory."
Deuteronomy 20:4

We were anxiously awaiting the pathology report from the surgery which, for this one, typically comes one week after the procedure. This report is used to determine if there are still viable cancer cells present in the breast tissue that was removed, and if so, how close those cells are to the margins of the skin. This helps the doctors decide if further treatment, such as radiation, is necessary.

So here I was again, watching my phone and waiting for it to ring. Waiting for news when you're living with a cancer diagnosis is excruciating, and the agony I felt when I waited months ago for the phone call from the radiologist after my biopsy, was creeping in again. It wasn't quite as intense as before because the circumstances were a little different now, and I had come pretty far from that initial information download, but I was still nervous. Every time my phone rang, I quickly checked the caller ID to see if it was the hospital. Finally, the call came, and I answered it on the first ring. I heard the voice of my nurse advocate on the other end and, she cut right to the chase. I could bore you with all of the fancy medical talk, but instead, I will give you the results in my own words…

"THE CANCER IS DEAD!!!"

Yep, like dead, dead. Dead as a doornail dead. The tumor was toast. ALL. OF. IT. Just like that, this journey that started with a phone call ended with a phone call. My nurse advocate's name, who delivered this incredible news, was Joy, and this beautiful detail was not lost on me. God is in the details and even now He was showing His love for me, not only with the amazing results and answered prayer, but also in who He had chosen to be the messenger.

It was a surreal feeling to be told that you no longer have cancer after living so deep in the trenches fighting for what seems like an eternity for that exact outcome. You don't know if you should laugh or cry, so you do both, and you sit in amazement at God's faithfulness and the unwavering fulfillment of His sweet promises. I had prayed for this exact outcome for months. I had prayed that there would be nothing left living in that tumor. I had prayed that the chemo had done its job and all of the struggle, loss of my physical strength, and emotional acrobatics, would be worth it. I was prepared for less than optimal results because I trusted God that He would bring me through this and that His plan was perfect, no matter what. But hearing the words, "The cancer is dead," was the icing on the cake. Oh, and remember how significant the number four had become throughout this journey? Well, I received this incredible news almost exactly four months to the day of that first horrible phone call that started this whole ball rolling.

So, there you have it. I could finally, confidently, and gratefully say, with tears streaming down my face….

I am cancer free!
Thank you, Jesus!

Photography: Dawn Witty

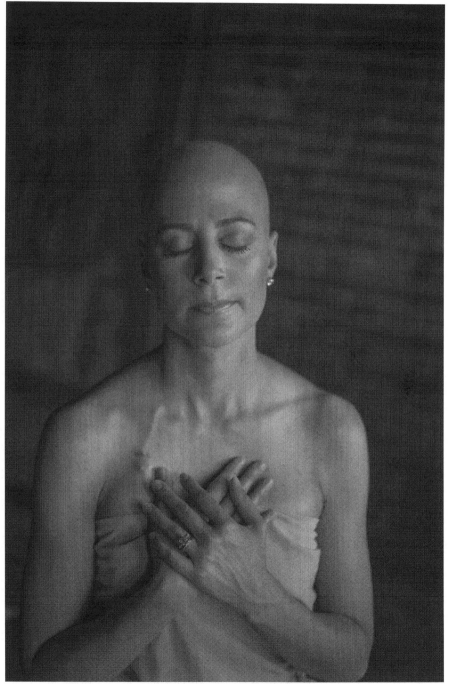

Photography by: Dahli Durley

Photography by: Dahli Durley

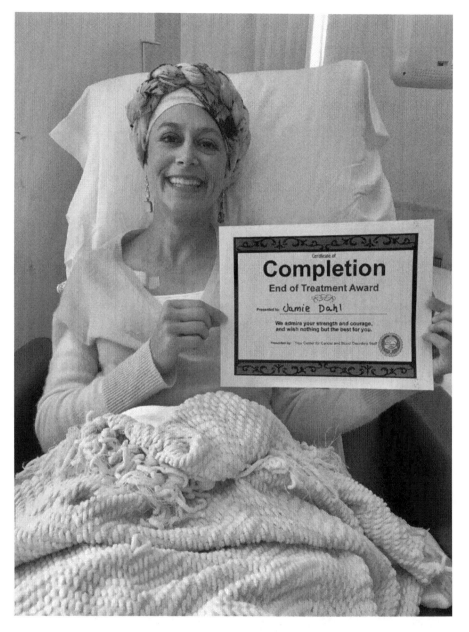

Photography: Dahli Durley

Part Two

Introduction

Breathe. With that incredible phone call and the happy news that I had so earnestly prayed for, I finally took a full, deep breath. As I did, I felt the weight of a cancer diagnosis begin to slowly lift. I was given permission to move on with my life and to put this horrible season behind me. But my work was not finished. There were lessons I had learned over those months that I needed to process, and others that I was just beginning to work through.

This next section contains what I call my "gems." Those valuable jewels of knowledge that I would never have gathered had I not experienced this trial. My story was not over. The hardest work was done, but this was where my inner transformations and the true ah-ha moments started to click. Most of these lesson gems are specific to the challenges faced during a battle with breast cancer. However, many could apply to any difficulty you may be experiencing. Remember those questions you wanted to ask earlier that I said we would get to? This is it. Pour another cup of coffee and let's get started.

26

Recovery: You Have to Pull Out the Big Guns

I was done. Or so I thought. Yes, the cancer was gone, and the pesky mouse in the corner of my barn was dead, but the barn was in shambles. That barn, my body, needed to be rebuilt and, as any building contractor would tell you, that doesn't happen overnight. It takes time to repair the rafters, the floor, rehang the doors, and paint the siding to make it look fresh again. But if you've ever gone through a construction or remodeling project, you can understand this. Once you are toward the end of the project and you've been living in the dust and mess for weeks or months, you are more than ready to have your life back, and your surroundings returned to some state of normal. It's very similar when you're recovering from cancer treatments. In my mind, I had completed my school assignment, and now I wanted to go out and play for recess! I struggled to wrap my head around the reality that this was not going to happen anytime soon. I still had a fight on my hands.

In my mind, I was ready to jump into normal "mom life" and start running all the errands that had accumulated over the past few months, completely organize and clean my house, and resume my role of a little kid taxi driver. But my body was saying, "Not so fast, sister!" And I had to listen. This meant giving myself some grace and learning to pace myself.

I found I would have days, or even weeks, where my energy level felt a bit more like my pre-cancer self, and I would take advantage of that, like a child given an unlimited spending limit at a toy store. I tried to run and "do" at my old pace because it felt good, and I felt like I was reclaiming my life again. However, if I pushed too hard for too long, I would experience what I coined a "crash day." My body would not so subtly tell me that enough was enough, and I would have to go straight to bed and sleep for twelve to thirteen hours.

This process took a long time, and there were days when I thought I may never feel like me again. However, the stretches between "crash days" slowly became longer, and I could feel my energy coming back bit by bit as time went on. If I had to put a time frame on this recovery season, I think it took me close to a year before the fatigue was gone and I was functioning at a level that felt familiar to ME.

Something that surprised me was how the change in routine would feel. By routine, I mean the constant doctor's appointments, infusion dates, and overall regular trips to the hospital. Over the course of this process, you get to know the nurses, physicians, front desk ladies, and the IV specialists pretty well. There is a familiarity that develops and friendships form. You get used to the repetitive nature of living your life at the hospital, and when that part is over, there is a strange void that occurs. Don't get me wrong. I was MORE than ready to be done with those appointments. I did a little happy dance when I left my last appointment, but when that routine is gone, there's a brief sense of, "What the heck do I do now?"

I think simply being aware of this, and realizing it's normal to feel a little lost when your schedule isn't pre-booked for you, is the best thing you can do. I found it helpful to slowly begin replacing those routines with other things that filled me up emotionally -- whether that was some time with a close friend over a cup of coffee or a weekly yoga class.

I also noticed that it took a few months for me to be able to walk back into the hospital for any type of appointment, either for myself or my children, without having a minor panic attack. My emotions were still very raw. It took some time for me to be able to sit in a doctor's office without my heart pounding out of my chest while mindlessly rattling off my name and date of birth, without being asked first. However, it did get better.

I remember that specific day when I walked through the revolving hospital entrance door, heading to one of my routine checkup appointments with my oncologist, and I had a calming sense of peace. My heart no longer pounded. My palms didn't get sweaty. And, I didn't fear that I wouldn't be able to walk back out of those hospital front doors after it was over and comfortably be on my way. It does get better, but it also takes time.

During this initial recovery season, I knew that there were three areas that I needed to focus on. I needed to address my physical, my mental, and my emotional health. Our overall well-being isn't solely based on one of these three areas. To feel whole, we need to be in tune with all three, while actively pouring into all of these buckets.

Imagine a child riding their tricycle around the driveway. If one or two of the tires are flat or wobbly, the bike is not going to function properly, and the child's bike ride will not be nearly as much fun as it could be. The same is true for us. We need to be equally balanced in all areas of our health or at least be working on those areas that need a little more attention. For example, after going through a massive physical assault like cancer, it's easy to forget or lose sight of the mental and emotional pieces of our lives. But these areas are also crucial to recovery and can't be overlooked.

Because the physical weakness was the most glaring area of need once I finished my treatments and surgery, that became the area I tried to tackle right away. Being relatively inactive, compared to my previous activity level, my muscles and heart were in sad disrepair. I had been faithful about taking short walks and doing light arm exercises after surgery, but overall, I was a weak wreak.

I can tell you that being a former dancer, I was having none of that. When our physical health is stolen from us, we realize just how important our health is, and it lights a fire under us to reclaim it. So, I got really excited about hitting an exercise routine as hard as my body would allow me to. I got involved with a wonderful program at our local YMCA, designed for cancer survivors and I slowly began to rebuild my cardiovascular health and my muscle strength. I felt like a rockstar walking through those gym doors, even though my treadmill level was pushing a one or two and I was breathing heavy after 10 minutes. But I was there, and I was making progress. The going was slow, but I continued to press ahead, listen to my body and take one day at a time. Even though it was sometimes difficult not to be hard on myself or get frustrated when I could only press or curl ten pounds, I learned to celebrate those ten pounds!

So, I'm speaking to all of you fellow overachievers and perfectionists out there. You have to learn to celebrate the small victories and be okay with things not always happening in your timing. My experience with trying to recover my physical health became a great learning lesson for me. I have a hard time when things don't happen when I want them to or what I deem to be quick enough. Now, I was smack dab in the middle of a situation where I didn't have much control over how fast my body healed. Could I do my part by eating healthily, exercising as much as was realistic for my condition, and rest when I needed to? Of course! But, ultimately how fast I bounced back, was up to God and my body. I had to trust in that process and embrace each step along the way.

Instead of getting frustrated when I had a crash day, I made a point to reflect on how many days had gone by since my last one. Or, count it as one more crash day closer to my last. Ultimately, it was an exercise of letting go of control. I had to trust and believe that God knows my body better than I do because He knit me in my mother's womb. He knows how fast or how slow it should take to heal, and it was my job to trust the process.

During those times when I got frustrated that the recovery wasn't going as fast as I would like, or when it felt like I was taking steps backward some days, I chose to combat those feelings with reflection. I went back to the encouraging notes, Bible verses, and experiences that God used to get me through the darkness. In doing that, my mind and spirit were flooded with a much-needed renewal and refreshing. God had brought me this far, and He wasn't going to leave me now. Was this next stage of my physical recovery going to take time, and was it going to be hard? Absolutely. But His promises of making beauty from ashes were still true. Hebrews 13:8 says: *"Jesus Christ is the same yesterday today and forever,"* so everything He brought me through yesterday is going to apply to today, and my future.

The other area I knew I needed to focus on was my mental health. People often talk about "chemo brain" and how the treatments can make you fuzzy and your mental processes feel slow. At first, I thought this term was just an excuse to hide normal forgetfulness, but holy cow, people! This is a real thing! There was one day back when I was in the thick of my chemo treatments when my father asked me to write down a grocery list so he could pick up some needed supplies for our family. He was always so wonderful and helpful with running those necessary errands. I was trying to write down "orange juice," and for the life of me, I couldn't remember how to spell the word, "orange!" It felt like someone had decorated the inside of my head for Halloween with fake cobwebs and every brain synapse was covered in sticky goo. Frustrating? Yes!

My thought processes became noticeably slower, and even basic math became a bit of a struggle at times. So, after I was done with the treatments, I began trying to retrain my brain to clear the cobwebs. I started taking it through its own exercise routine, and I would even challenge it with some mental gymnastics. One exercise I practiced was visualizing myself driving to places in my community and then trying to remember street signs or landmarks along the way.

I also made a point to engage with people in conversation and tried to really focus and remember things they were saying. I practiced basic math equations in my head and worked on adding up prices of items while I was shopping. Playing cards or games with the girls became helpful, too. Over time, I could feel the fog lift, and my normal brain function started to reappear. I have to admit that I will still, unapologetically, pull the "chemo brain" card when I say something dumb or forget an appointment. Hey, don't judge! I earned the right to use that card, and I'm going to milk it for as long as humanly possible! But once again, I had to give myself the green light to be okay with not having it all together, mentally, and trust that God would restore my mind in time.

The other area I focused on was my emotional health. Our emotional health is probably the most complex piece when it comes to recovering from a traumatic experience. I was finally seeing the light at the end of the tunnel and could slowly see myself emerging from this bunker that I had been entrenched in, fighting for my life. At the same time, I began to feel incredible grief. I was mourning all I had lost: my physical strength, my hair, quality time with my children, just to name a few, and even though I was thankfully very alive, I was grieving as though something, or someone, had died.

Throughout the process, I experienced all of the stages of the grief cycle: denial, anger, bargaining, depression, and acceptance, and each of these stages would pop up at different times. I grieved for what I had been through and what my family had endured. It wasn't until I was in the clear and had been given that clean bill of health that I was finally able to reflect on everything that had just happened and begin processing the loss.

The other incredibly important role that your emotional health plays during trials is your mindset. I can't stress enough the importance of trying to stay positive, not only during the recovery phase but also when you're in the thick of the storm. The feelings of fear and doubt that kept creeping in telling me that I was never going to escape this life sentence continually, tried to take hold in my heart. But when I took a stand against the lies and used my mind, my words, and my prayers to fight back, those lies began to lose precious ground.

Our minds and our thoughts have incredible power, and when you can take your thoughts captive it is a game changer! Proverbs 23:7 says, *"As a man thinks, so he is."* You can choose to dwell on negative thoughts, fears, and doubt or you can choose to believe in your heart and say with your mouth that you are going to get through this! Speaking life and light out loud to yourself has a way of freeing yourself from the bondage of negativity. Stand in front of your bathroom mirror, look yourself in the eyes, and say, "I am going to be fine. God has a plan and a purpose for my life, and I am going to get to the other side of this trial." You may feel silly or slightly crazy at first, but l promise, that if you make this a practice, your mindset will follow suit.

Another way I combatted depression was through music. I love music, and when I listen to a good song, whether it's a rocking track from my favorite Prince album or a beautiful song from the contemporary Christian group, Hillsong, something touches me deep in my soul. For me, music is great on all levels, but it's life-changing when it comes in the form of worship. Worship may be a foreign concept for you, and that's okay.

Worship is the act of expressing reverence and adoration for God. It's being before Him and simply listening, meditating, or belting out a song that praises Him. Especially on those days when I didn't have much fight left in me, if I cranked up some praise and worship music and simply sat in God's presence with my mind focused on Him and Him alone, I could feel soothing happening in my heart. It felt like balm for my soul. The act of worship takes the focus off of ourselves and onto God and opens up a pathway for healing on so many levels. It is another way to remind us of God's goodness and His love for us, no matter what we are going through. Often, certain song lyrics can become mantras that act as depression busters and myth destroyers when we are sinking into those dark places. So, grab your headphones or crank up your in-home sound system and shift your energies to the heavens. You'll feel a shift in your heart, too.

To fight the negative, doomsday thoughts, I also made it a practice to visualize my future. Especially during those times when I felt horrible or particularly sad, I would imagine what I was going to be doing one year from that day. I would picture myself sitting by the pool with the girls drinking iced tea and playing with them in the water. I imagined what my hair was going to look like and what type of cute pixie style or bob it might be at that time. I daydreamed about busy days of running errands and meeting friends for lunch and imagined exactly what those moments were going to look like.

I used those scenarios as weapons against the battle that was raging in my head. I also used my most important piece of ammunition which was scripture. Isaiah 54:17 says, *"No weapon that is formed against you will prosper..."*

Jeremiah 29:11 states, *"For I know the plans I have for you,"* declares the Lord, *"plans to prosper you and not to harm you, plans to give you hope and a future."* When you use scripture to fight your battles, you are officially pulling out the big guns, and any soldier will tell you that when you're in the heat of the battle, it would be foolish to forget about the arsenal that is sitting right beside you.

27

But I'm So Afraid

The emotion that I think has the highest potential to take us out is fear. Fear paralyzes. Fear tells us that there is no hope or future, and it binds us in chains that keep us from going where we are called to go. A cancer diagnosis is just one example of how fear can take root in our lives and potentially derail us. As I waited for the results of that first biopsy, it was fear that crippled me. I was instantly afraid of the unknown and the terrifying path that was opening itself to me, like the gaping jaws of a horrifying monster. Just the possibility that I might have cancer froze me in my tracks and fear was the culprit.

Fear's best friend is the loss of control. Those two scoundrels like to hang out together, arm-in-arm, on the street corner heckling us with lies, trying to convince us that our situation is hopeless. When we believe that we, alone, can fix our problems because we are strong enough or smart enough, it creates an unhealthy breeding ground for fear. When that control is stripped away, and we realize that we can't do this life on our own and that we may have to surrender to something greater than ourselves, fear begins to take center stage. It lies to us and tells us that we are never going to get through this and that our world is going to come crashing down. It tells us that there is no hope for repair or renewal. But again, this is where we need to fight.

The first step is surrendering ourselves to the idea that, yes, this may be a situation that we can't fix, and we are going to have to surrender our will and our life to the God that gave us life. We may actually need to trust in someone that we may not be able to physically see, but who knows exactly how many hairs are on our head. Or, in my case, NOT on my head. It's not easy to open our hands and relinquish that control, but only in doing this will we find true freedom and peace.

When we are struggling with fear, it's very easy to fill our mind and our thoughts with a lot of "what ifs." What if I don't recover? What if my kids are scarred for life? What if my marriage suffers? What if cancer comes back? Going to the "what if" scenario is very normal when life isn't ice cream sundaes and cuddly puppies. "What if" is the evil spawn of worry and if we allow ourselves to go down that path, we will end up creating even worse scenarios in our mind that begin to spiral out of control. Pretty soon the sky is falling, our world is crumbling, and we are completely and utterly hopeless. I am guilty of traveling down the "what if" road, myself, and it's not a pretty place to be. But "what if" has its own form of kryptonite that will melt it like water over the Wicked Witch of the West. Are you ready for it? Here it is… "I AM."

Let's go back to our favorite, initially insecure, and slightly fearful, Bible Hall of Famer, Moses. Moses had an encounter with God at a burning bush that changed the course of his life forever. In Exodus 3, the story begins with Moses leisurely taking care of a flock of sheep. Then he saw a bush that was burning, yet it wasn't consumed. God began to speak to Moses from the bush, giving him specific direction to take on the seemingly impossible task of leading the enslaved Israelite people out of Egypt and away from the powerful captor, Pharaoh. Moses' response is classic. He essentially says, "God, who, in your green earth, am **I** to do this huge task?"

Here is that fear and doubt thing kicking in. God responds with reassuring Moses that He will be with him the entire time. But do you think Moses took that answer and said, "Cool! Let's rock this! Here I come Pharaoh!" Nope, he responded with another question that I will paraphrase in what I like to imagine sounded a little like this, "God, when I tell the Israelites that YOU want them to pack up, call some Ubers, and head out of town, I know they're going to think I am completely off my rocker. They're going to want to know Your name, and what do I tell them?" Here is God's response in Exodus 3:14, "...*I AM THAT I AM...*" Then God proceeds to give Moses a play-by-play on how the mission will be victorious and how HE will do mighty things to ensure that Moses will succeed in his task.

Now, I wasn't there with Moses at the burning bush, but if I were, I would bet that he was experiencing a lot of "what if's" going through his head. "What if the Israelite people don't want to leave Egypt? What if Pharaoh never agrees to let them go? What if I walk into that palace and the guards eat me for lunch? Bottom line. What. If. I. Fail?" We are all a lot like Moses, and this is often our first reaction when presented with impossible or hopeless situations. But if we can train our thoughts to replace the "what if" scenarios with "I AM" and trust that God will make a way then we will begin to feel the power that we have when we put our faith in God. The outcome may not look like what we think it will look like, or it may take a lot longer than we would prefer, but God is faithful and will see us through to the end.

So yes, fear is a huge struggle that we all deal with when going through trials. Was I afraid while going through my trial? Heck, yes! But I fought hard against that fear and pulled out my weapons when the battle started to heat up. My weapon of choice was Joshua 1:9 which also happens to be our family verse. "*Have I not commanded you? Be strong and courageous. Do not be afraid; do not be discouraged, for the Lord your God will be with you wherever you go.*"

My kids know this verse by heart, and we have it written on a chalkboard by our backdoor to look at and read every morning as we leave the house. We all experience fear at times, and sometimes it's intense, but there is a God that can bind that fear with chains that can't be broken. Then He will bring us into a place of peace if we allow ourselves to trust and let go of the wheel.

28

Where is Your Strength?

One of the things I heard very frequently from people when I was first diagnosed, was "Be strong!" As time went on, when I was in the thick of my fight, those words morphed into "YOU are so strong." I was incredibly grateful for the encouragement and cheering on from my friends and family, but being the people pleaser that I am, there were times when I allowed that phrase to put me under pressure. By no means do I fault people for telling me that, in fact, as I mentioned earlier, it was empowering, and I know it was said out of love, but unfortunately, I often allowed myself to take a twisted approach to it. That approach was one of self-imposed expectations that I knew I couldn't meet all on my own.

There were days when I definitely did feel strong. I put on a brave face, and my fashionista head wraps with a "fight like a girl" attitude. But there were also days when I wasn't so strong. Those were the days when all I wanted to do was crawl in a hole, sob like a baby, raise my white flag, and give up. I'll be honest, I felt a little guilty that I was letting myself, or my loved ones, down because I wasn't bucking up, pulling my weight and being "strong." In those moments, I was definitely not the poster child for inner strength. In fact, I felt like a full-on failure, and that is where that erroneous perception that we have to fight our battles completely on our own, begins to take over. But guess what? We can't do this crazy life on our own, and we're not supposed to. Stop putting that kind of pressure on yourself and learn to give yourself a little grace.

This is the best part. Are you ready? You CAN be that incredibly tough person that faces a battle with a steely gaze and solid determination because you have a God who loves you and desires to show His mighty power in your weaknesses. 2 Corinthians 12:9 says, "*My grace is sufficient for you, for my power is made perfect in weakness.*" The Oxford Dictionary defines the word power as "the ability or capacity to do something or act in a particular way."

When you feel like you can't do anymore or fix whatever darkness you're experiencing, remember that God can. He will use that opportunity to pour out His power over you and your life and manifest Himself in ways you never could think or imagine. I don't believe that He enjoys seeing our weakness, but I do believe He gets a bit excited when we acknowledge our need for Him.

I imagine Him sitting on the edge of His heavenly throne waiting for us to throw up our hands in surrender, and when we finally do, He leans back, puts His hands behind His head and says, "Alright, let's do this." Being the loving Father that He is, He excitedly gets to work pouring out His mighty power into our lives and manifesting His goodness through those areas of weakness.

When you tap into the strength of God, it's like being transported into one of my favorite scenes from the movie, Wonder Woman, starring the actress, Gal Gadot. I always get a little "goosebumpy" when I watch it. It begins with Wonder Woman walking in the trenches during a battle in World War I where the soldiers are fighting over "no man's land." No man's land is a span of territory that the allies have not been able to breach due to the heavy fire from the enemy, but Gal Gadot's Wonder Woman character sees the desperate need of the trapped villagers beyond the enemy lines, and bravely climbs the ladder out of the trench.

She begins to cross the desolate area, taking fire and deflecting bullets as she slowly, but assertively, walks straight into the enemy's attack. Then she kneels down, pulling her shield in front of her, as the bullets cascade off of it making way for the troops behind her to charge. Due to her courage and resolve, the soldiers ultimately succeed in crossing a landscape that seemed, until this point, completely impenetrable.

You have the power with God as your shield, to walk with confidence and determination through the battles that come your way, but you simply need to surrender to the fact that you need His strength and His power to do it. You must take that first, maybe terrifying, step out of the safe zone and face those fears. But you're not alone if you lead with the shield of the Holy Spirit, which is strong enough to fend off any bullets that may come flying at you. When you trust in God's ability to go before you, then yes, you can confidently say, "I AM STRONG."

29

Give Yourself a Break

It's okay to have bad days. It's okay to say, "You know what? This really stinks and I don't think I can make it through this." It's important to stop trying to perform for others to convince them you're handling this just fine. Find those people you trust and let them see your vulnerability, and your weakness. When you're able to share that weakness, it opens a door for your friends and loved ones to come around you and hold you up. They will be the ones, along with God, to remind you that you can do this, and you are going to get to the other side. It doesn't mean you're a failure. It simply means you're human.

Maybe you're not recovering as fast as you think you should after your treatments. Or maybe because of everything you're dealing with right now, you forgot to send a snack with your child to school again, for the second day in a row. (I've never done this. Only read about it.) It's okay. I sometimes feel like I have to be that perfect cross between Martha Stewart, June Cleaver, and the CEO of Apple Inc., but that just isn't reality. Yes, I may have a Pinterest win, once in a while, and the super cute brownie treats I made for the second-grade class shaped and colored like Legos, turned out beautifully. However, the majority of the time, I'm just trying to keep my kids physically alive and in relatively clean clothes. Couple that with fighting off a deadly disease and it's a recipe for disaster.

So, give yourself a break! You don't have to be all things for all people, especially when you're struggling through a difficult time. It's about giving yourself grace. Grace defined, as it relates to the Christian faith, is the unmerited favor and love of God. It's a gift that we don't deserve but is poured out on us, regardless.

This is how God loves you when you believe and trust in Him. I had to learn to relate this same concept to myself. I am one of those people that can be particularly hard on myself if I don't measure up to my self-imposed expectations. I needed to learn how to take "me" off the hook and give myself some unmerited favor. If the dishes didn't get done, it was okay. If the house looked like a tornado had ripped through it twice, it was okay. If the kids ate macaroni and cheese for the third night in a row, it was okay. Taking that pressure off and replacing it with grace, released me to settle into a better state of peace that I had been horribly lacking.

It's also important to give yourself the grace to acknowledge frustration if things aren't going your way and in your timing. But at the same time, be constantly reminding, yourself, that God never fails and this season will pass. When you're fighting those unrealistic expectations, just remember to give yourself one simple word. Grace.

30

Preparing Your Heart to Lose Your Hair

Losing my hair was one of the things I was most afraid of when I was diagnosed. I know that may seem incredibly conceited, but as a woman, our hair is a comfort. Typically, we think being bald is super cute on a little baby or downright sexy if you are blessed to be Vin Diesel. But for an average gal like myself, it's not exactly a "hairstyle choice" I have dreamt about all my life, that I'd like to give a whirl. So, when you're faced with the reality that it's all going to go, it's truly heartbreaking.

There are definite stages that I found myself going through during this process and, for me, who is a consummate planner, it was difficult not being able to have a plan for how I was going to deal with this. I realized I had to just go with the flow. I would need to figure it out along the way.

As I had mentioned earlier, the achy "ponytail in too long" feeling was a dead giveaway, and that was exactly what it felt like when it all started to go. It was only a few days after I had that feeling that those poor little follicles started releasing their precious possessions. Once I decided to shave my head down to a buzz cut to spare both my family and my vacuum cleaner from the mess of a massive long hair fall-out, I was left with shorter half inch strands that then continued to come out over time. It was a bit depressing seeing my remaining hair continue to quickly disappear. I traveled from the stage of actually liking my freshly buzzed cut and feeling pretty sassy, to a depressed stage as I watched my cute look turn into a haphazard mess.

I had massive bald spots around my temples and the back of my head where it rubbed while I slept, but there were still a handful of stragglers that wouldn't let go, and boy, were they stubborn. It made me look like a one-hundred-year-old woman who had just crawled out of a cave, and it was driving me crazy. I couldn't stand this in-between stage of being "kinda-sorta" bald, so I decided to do something about it.

Someone I had been sharing this dilemma with, gave me a crazy idea about what another cancer patient, who was struggling with this same issue, was doing. They had taken duct tape and gently pressed it on their head then pulled it off removing the remaining little stubborn suckers. This sounded absolutely asinine to me, but guess what? I did it. I know, I know, it seems like medieval torture, and my physician is probably cringing right now, but honestly, it worked like a charm! It didn't even hurt! I was able to gently remove the rest of the hair so I could fully step into that next stage of being completely bald. For some reason, I needed to be there both for my mental state and my physical state. The in-between stage was honestly more torturous for me than sticking almost an entire roll of duct tape on my scalp.

I also never realized just how cold you get when you have no hair! This all happened to me during the early spring months, so thankfully, I was coming into a warmer season, but even with Mother Nature on my side, I still got cold. I found that having a little cap to wear to bed at night, or even pulling the covers up over my head, so only my face stuck out, was very soothing. Thankfully scarves and hats were my friends, and that helped battle the daily chill.

Many women also struggle with whether or not they are going to wear a wig. I went back and forth on this and, at one point, was actually pretty excited about trying out some sassy new hairstyles and finally getting to live out my dream of being an undercover agent, like in the movies, who has a blonde shag one day and then sexy, black, curly tresses the next. In my crazy state of mind, I actually even had the thought that I could rock a hot pink bob and somehow make it seem cool. Yeah, that lasted about two seconds.

I jumped on the internet and started ordering all kinds of wigs in different shapes, colors, and sizes. It would have been way better to actually go into a nice wig shop and try some on to see if wigs were even "me", but I live in a small town where the majority of wigs I could find were in the costume section of the party supply store and better suited for Alice in Wonderland or a naughty nurse.

When the box arrived with my wigs, flown in from a store in Los Angeles, I got super excited and ran to the mirror to try them on. I was sure I was going to feel like Angelina Jolie or Jennifer Lopez, but when I put them on and straightened the flyaways, I literally laughed out loud. Nope. I'm definitely not a wig girl. I have seen many women look absolutely stunning wearing them, and wigs are wonderful for helping many women feel confident and beautiful, but for me, I knew it wasn't a match. But I also realized something else. It was good for me to go through this process.

If you are facing the reality that you are going to lose your hair because of cancer treatments, I think it's good to explore all options when it comes to how you're going to deal with the baldness. Try some different styles of hats. Buy some gorgeous scarves. Do some experimenting with them in front of the mirror with a girlfriend and a good smoothie. Or get a variety of wigs and see if one makes you feel like a million bucks. You don't know until you try. Once you do, you will see exactly what makes you feel good, and you will have more self-assurance walking out this difficult stage and a tad more confidence in your step.

It's not forever! This was something I had to remind myself every day. I knew there would be a time when my hair would grow back, and I remember thinking it would be the day after my last treatment. Well, that didn't happen exactly, but I would be lying if I didn't check my scalp for any sign of intelligent life within the first few weeks after I was done with chemo. It took at least two months for me to have some visible growth, and enough of it, for me to feel comfortable in public without one of my scarf turbans. Remember, everyone is unique, and hair grows differently, and at different rates, so my experience may not be yours.

What surprised me the most as it started growing back, was how my scalp felt! It felt as though the hairs were breaking through the surface for the first time and my skin felt like an inside out cactus. It was slightly painful and wearing hats actually hurt a little. This eventually passed, but even though my scalp was tender, I couldn't help but rub my head ALL THE TIME. It felt so good to have those little prickly newbies finally poking through, and all I wanted to do was pet them and tell them to keep growing nice and strong!

Another thing I made a point of doing, while my hair was growing back, was to take pictures of each stage. The crazy thing is, the stages literally change overnight! I would just begin to master the spiky punk look with the help of my husband's hair products and invaluable styling tips, and then the next morning the spiky punk look would be old news. It would be replaced with some other bizarre mop of indescribable weirdness to work with. It actually became quite fun.

The best morning came early in my hair growing saga when I woke up, sleepily shuffled to my bathroom, and looked in the mirror. I immediately noticed something strange protruding from the back of my head just behind my ear. What in the world is that? Oh my gosh. It's bed head. I actually have some hairs that are long enough to stick up in the back. HALLELUJAH, PEOPLE! I HAVE BED HEAD!! You have to celebrate the little things.

As I navigated this crazy world of becoming a living and breathing Chia Pet, I had fun making comparisons between my changing hairstyles and celebrities or known entertainment characters. My new hair decided it wanted to be the poster child for "chemo curl" and initially came in like Shirley Temple on steroids. I went through the Hugh Jackman as Wolverine stage and made my rounds through many of Jim Carrey's characters, from Lloyd Christmas in *Dumb and Dumber* to Ace Ventura in the *Pet Detective* movies. I'm currently working on a mashup between Princess Diana and Hillary Clinton, at the moment.

Getting that first haircut was almost like getting one as a child. I was nervous and excited and really hoping for the lollipop afterward. I was hesitant to cut it at all because I had gone through so much to grow what I had so far, but I knew it was smart to do a little trimming in the back to help the sides catch up a bit. I like to call it "mullet management." Because the hair comes in baby fine and soft like it did when we were infants, I was so nervous about doing any blow drying for fear of damaging it somehow. It probably would have been fine, but up until this point, I had really shied away from giving it some heat. But in the trusted hands of my hairdresser, I let her blow it out straight for the first time. It was barely long enough to do so, but when she started to work on the section around my face, I looked in the mirror and started to cry. It was as if I could see my old self again for just a split second. All of the emotions and feelings of loss of my former self exploded over that hairdryer and round brush, but it felt really good to say, "Welcome back!" to that person I thought I had lost forever.

I feel like it takes longer than you would like for your hair to come back, but I found that celebrating each stage and embracing it for what it is, can actually be pretty fun. I also found that my daughters reacted to my hair loss and regrowth very differently. My oldest didn't seem to mind the drastic changes too much or at least didn't express it through her words, but often asked me to tie turbans on her head to match mine, instead. She also wanted to cut her long hair into a short bob as I was growing mine out, which I could tell was also a coping mechanism for her.

My youngest, on the other hand, was very vocal about how sad she was to see me without my hair. She missed my long hair very much and would frequently express that sentiment on many a random occasion. Coincidentally enough, she became slightly obsessed with growing her own hair "to her feet," Crystal Gayle style.

I honored their feelings and listened when they needed to talk about it. I also continued to remind them that I was the same person, with or without hair, and tried to model being confident in all stages. My hope was that they would learn that it's okay to take pride in our appearance and feel comfortable in our own skin, no matter what, but to not find our identity or self-worth in things like our hair. Watching the two of them go through this, was fascinating and showed me how children process things so differently. You have to tailor your responses and reactions for each one according to their emotional makeup and continue to be positive and upbeat about it all.

Bottom line is hair, although it may feel like it defines you, is only a decoration. The true beauty is inside the package and inside of you. It's not sitting on top of your head. The bow on the package may be gone momentarily, but it will come back, and either way, YOU ARE BEAUTIFUL.

31

Take the Help

No matter what your situation is in life, there are going to be times when you may need a little help. How many times did we reach for our mother's hand as children while crossing a busy street or trying to tie our shoelaces? Just because we are adults doesn't mean that we are free from the need of a little assistance once in a while. We may not be children, but we are still human and very much need a strong hand to reach for at times.

Please, please let yourself accept help. I know this can be a very difficult thing for some people because it may imply that we can't hack it or that we are weak. It takes a strong person to ask for help. It takes a strong and humble person to accept it. Make a conscious decision to break up with your prideful self. Start courting that humble part of you that opens up your hands and receives freely. By allowing people to help you, it not only takes the pressure off of you, but it also gives that person desiring to help a chance to serve.

There are many people whose love language is service. By allowing them to help, you are not only giving them an opportunity to exercise the God-given giftings that they have, but you're also letting God support and love you through individuals who are willing to be His hands and feet. So, take that casserole or kind offer to walk your dog. Breathe a little easier, knowing that there are people who have been specifically put in your path to lighten your load.

You might be thinking of someone right now who is going through a difficult time. You may be wondering what you can do to help. This is something that many people struggle with and was a comment I heard a lot when I was going through my treatments. The desire is there to help, but along with that comes an intense feeling of helplessness. It's difficult to relate to what someone needs, especially if you have never experienced whatever trial that person is going through. Here is some advice. Keep it simple and put yourself in their shoes. Try to anticipate a need that they may not even realize they have. Here are a few great examples of that.

It was around Easter when I began my first chemo treatments, and I was beginning to feel a bit stressed and anxious about how I was going to get the girls' Easter baskets put together. I always enjoyed finding fun spring goodies and treats to stuff in their Pottery Barn, Peter Rabbit themed, monogrammed baskets, but I knew this year I wasn't going to have the energy to get out and shop for them. I didn't want this sweet time of year to feel drastically different for them because of my illness, but I worried that these little touches that had become part of our tradition would be missed because of my abysmal health.

However, just when I was feeling particularly worried and trying to figure out how I was going to make this happen, my sister-in-law dropped off two bags full of toys, candy-stuffed plastic eggs, and everything else I would need to make the girls' baskets look full and festive. All I had to do was dig their baskets out from the depths of my basement storage room, and fill them up. I can't tell you the burden that was lifted from me with just this small gesture. I never mentioned to her that I needed help with this. She simply anticipated a basic need that blessed me beyond words.

There are so many other ways you can help someone who is struggling. For example, right before I began my chemo treatments, my other sister-in-law dropped off a basket for me with comforting goodies like healthy snacks and a few fun fashion magazines. The basket also included a lightweight and cozy blanket that I ended up taking with me to every infusion appointment. It was the personal touch of each of these items and the thought that went into choosing them, that filled my bucket.

Another close friend gathered a small group of ladies, who showed up at my home on a cold, rainy day, and planted flowers in my planter boxes and outdoor pots. I sat on my couch, intermittently napping, and watching them from the window, as they made my view beautiful. My friend knew how important being able to see flowers was to me, and how healing that would be for my soul. The fruit of these few hours spent serving me in this way lasted the entire summer as I spent time outside breathing in the fresh air, resting, and enjoying this simple act of kindness.

My father was a faithful companion who would sit with me during my chemotherapy infusions or stay downstairs while I took a nap just so I had the comfort of knowing someone was nearby. He made frequent runs to the grocery store and kept our refrigerator full, so we didn't have to worry about that responsibility. My mother did many of the same things and also entertained my girls by getting them out of the house and doing some baking with grandma. The ways that my parents, and my in-laws, supported me are endless, but them simply being there was incredibly helpful and comforting all at the same time.

My husband's uncle, and wife cooked healthy plant-based meals for us every weekend and left them on our porch. We looked forward to that beautiful full cooler every Thursday, knowing that our time wouldn't have to be spent in the kitchen all weekend. Instead, we could eat a wonderful meal, rest, and use that time to connect with each other.

Whatever you do to anticipate someone's need doesn't have to be monumental. It can be simply shoveling a sidewalk in the winter or walking their dog. It's dropping off homemade bone broth or taking their kids to the pool for the day. Maybe it is organizing a meal train or a house cleaning schedule that you and a few friends can participate in together. It's what I like to call, simple serving, but it makes a big impact.

If you are in a place where you are realizing you need some help, then take a moment to think and write down your needs authentically. Do you need some meals brought in or someone to pick up some items on your grocery list for you? Maybe you're in desperate need of some time to truly rest in peace and quiet. That means scheduling a babysitter on a regular basis or asking a friend to watch your children every Wednesday until you're back on your feet. Or use that time to go to your favorite park or coffee shop, and absorb yourself in a good book for some mental rejuvenation.

Make sure you are identifying your needs and being real with yourself. This is a time when you need to put a plan in place to create an environment where you can most effectively heal, both physically and emotionally. Once you have that plan, then it's up to you to actually reach out to those people who will be willing participants in making that plan become a reality. Then you need to be content with allowing them to implement it.

32

What About My Kids?

The first thought I had, that scary day when the radiologist suspected cancer and told me that she was recommending a biopsy, was about my daughters. My mind swirled with questions. What would happen to them if this disease took my life? How would they react to us telling them about cancer and, ultimately, how would this tragedy affect their lives both now, and in the future? As a parent, it's obviously very natural to be incredibly concerned about our children and the effect that something difficult may have on them. But it's also important to remember that these precious little souls have been put into our care for a reason.

God has entrusted them specifically to YOU, and for a particular purpose. Our role, as a parent, is to be their guide through life. To further illustrate this point, I want you to get a little creative with me. Imagine you have decided to embark on an adventure of a lifetime and have chosen to climb Mt. Everest. Unless you are a highly trained and experienced mountain climber, you are probably not going to attempt to accomplish this feat on your own. Therefore, you will most likely hire a professional climbing guide whose job is to safely take you to the top of the mountain and back down with oodles of perfect selfies, a sweet t-shirt, and a mug to further document and celebrate the achievement.

That guide has a very important responsibility. They know that this climb is difficult and can be treacherous, but they also know they have an end goal to reach. Reaching that goal is going to mean a lot of hard work on the climber's part, possibly some sore and achy bodies, fatigue, and overall discomfort. But this is all part of the journey.

The guide isn't going to build a heated gondola, stocked with hot chocolate, that travels from the base of the mountain to the summit for the climbers to have a comfortable ride. That would defeat the purpose of the climb. It would take away the opportunity for them to experience challenge and pain, and to ultimately push through it and learn from it. It would rob them of the accomplishment they would feel when they finally reach the summit, and the lessons they learned along the way. It would steal from them the wisdom they will gain by persevering through the challenge themselves and then ultimately be able to share that wisdom with future climbers. The same goes with being a parent and guiding children through life's challenges.

We can be that kind of parent that wraps our kids in proverbial bubble wrap and protects them from any and all pain, or we can see difficulties as a chance to model for them ways to cope and survive. You will be surprised just how strong and resilient your children can be. Allowing them to go through the process with you, gives them a safe place to learn and work through their feelings. But this doesn't just happen on its own. As their parent and their guide, you need to be intentional about it.

Keep the communication lines open, and always be willing to listen. The times when they want to talk may not be most convenient for you, but you have to roll with it. I'm the person that typically needs a lot of sleep and will turn into a pumpkin when the clock strikes nine at night. However, this is the time that my oldest daughter likes to talk. It's when she's snuggled in her bed, and I'm sitting beside her, saying our prayers that she begins to open up. Inside I'm DYING because I can barely see straight, and all I can imagine at that moment is crawling into my bed and passing out. However, this is her moment, and as her mom, I have to suck it up, get over myself, and press into this sweet time with her.

Asking questions to get a conversation started is helpful and not being afraid to ask them those tough questions, is important. They want you, as their parent, to be real with them. They don't want the smoke and mirrors and the sugarcoated fluffy answers. They are searching for truth and you, as their parent, should be the one to provide them with that. Now don't get me wrong, these conversations should always be age appropriate, and only you know your children best when it comes to how to approach them with sensitive information.

For example, my daughters were six and almost eight years old during my diagnosis, and we tiptoed around the fact that I could lose my life due to this disease. We stressed the severity of it, but for us, we didn't feel comfortable going to that extreme with them while I was going through it. After it was all over, we talked more about that reality and the possibility that this disease could have taken my life, and for us, that decision worked best for our girls.

Giving your children the tools they need to cope with stress is important, too. Prayer was the biggest tool in our toolbox. We prayed with our girls regularly. My husband and I let them see, or "catch us" praying together all the time. We talked about our faith in God and that we believe that He has the power to heal. Countless times I shared scripture that I received from friends with them and explained my feelings and how that particular scripture filled my heart at that moment. I talked freely about the amazing things I felt God was doing in my life during that time and we celebrated those moments. I wanted them to experience the realness of God in a situation that was all too real for them. Teaching them to notice God in the little and big moments, while they are young, will set them up to notice Him more as they grow older. It will help them realize the beauty of having a personal relationship with Jesus.

Good carpenters can't build a house with only a hammer, so it's important to stock our little ones' tool belts with other tools to help them cope. As I mentioned early in my story, our daughters participated in a program at the hospital put on by the wonderful staff of social workers. It was a full day of games, discussions, art projects and tours of the oncology center. It was designed to help them express their feelings and their fears in a third-party setting. Enlisting the help of licensed professionals who are trained to talk to children about cancer or any other trial or trauma, is important. They have the experience that many of us parents don't have and are able to give us tips and ideas to help our children through a difficult time.

I also informed my girls' teachers at school what was going on. It was pretty obvious with my bald head that there were some major things happening to our family. I highly doubted that the staff just thought I was going through a Sinead O'Connor wannabe phase, so I felt it was important to explain. The teachers were wonderful and supported the girls beautifully. We wanted them to feel comfortable sharing their feelings with their teachers if they felt the need to do so. Giving them every opportunity to communicate what was going on in their minds and hearts, was important to us.

Connecting them with peers that can relate to their experience is also helpful. Going through a family trial, as a child, can feel very isolating. If they can talk with or play with another child, who has either gone through the same thing or something similar, can bring a much-needed emotional connection. Sometimes just knowing that they're not alone and that another child has gone through it, too, can give them some peace and confidence that everything is going to be okay.

Staying upbeat and positive is important for children to see. Can you let them see you be sad once in a while, or cry with them when everyone is having a particularly bad day? Absolutely. But overall, you should try to make a strong effort to always give them hope. Think about the mountain climbing guide again. If he and his climbers are halfway up the mountain and a horrible snowstorm rolls in, threatening to take them all out, do you think he would say, "OMG! We're all going down!" I highly doubt it. This would only send the novice climbers into a state of panic, and any level thinking would go out the window. No, that guide would stay calm, give the climbers orders and instructions of how to weather the storm, and continue to encourage them that they will make it through the threatening conditions. The same goes with parenting your children through a crisis.

Stay calm, give them instructions, communicate and, most importantly, listen to them. They will follow your lead.

My hope for my girls, after living through my fight with cancer, is that this experience will change them for the better. My prayer is that they will have more compassion for others experiencing pain and that they will have a stronger sense of empathy. I also hope that they will look back on this when they are older and struggling with their own trials, that they remember that they persevered. That we stayed the course as a family and no matter what the outcome, we were going to stick together and keep putting one foot in front of the other.

Trees that are planted where they are forced to endure moderate to strong winds, end up growing stronger and straighter than those that never experience being bent and stressed. I want my children to have a strong trunk, and even stronger roots so that their lives will be fruitful and able to withstand the even harsher winds that will come in their future. Maybe this will change the course of their lives, and maybe their path will lead them into the medical field with a strong desire to help others. The outcome is not for me to say, but as a parent, it is more than I can ask for if their momentary struggle ultimately builds their character and potentially opens up a door for them to step more fully into the plan and purpose that God has for them.

33

Don't Compare!

One of the things that I think a lot of women struggle with is comparison. I have to say that I have fallen into this category more times than I'd like to admit, and it's not a fun place to be. I feel that by nature we are constantly looking at others and then back at ourselves to see how we measure up. Living in a society where social media feeds this problem doesn't help either. There have been countless times when I have just gotten off an Instagram or Facebook scrolling binge and felt like my clothes were boring, my make-up was pathetic, and that my kids were all hot messes.

I felt this way because I was comparing my life to the seemingly perfect lives of all of those other people out there that, in reality, probably have some boring clothes and hot mess kids once in a while, too. The big old meanie, otherwise known as "comparison," loves to materialize and rear his ugly head when it comes to going through trials, too.

When you're diagnosed with a disease as common as breast cancer, it's very easy to start looking at other people's experience and to compare it to yours. But I would highly encourage anyone who is struggling with this, or just beginning their breast cancer journey, to run like the wind from this tendency! First of all, in terms of breast cancer, there are so many varying diagnoses. Between the different types of cancer cell receptors, to the size of the tumor, to the involvement and stages, the combinations seem endless. What one person may experience for their treatment plan and recovery, may not be what you will experience.

One area that is easy to begin comparing yourself to is the physical aspect of going through treatments. I remember when I was first diagnosed, I reached out to ladies who I knew were cancer survivors and had experienced chemotherapy. I had pages of questions for them because I wanted to prepare myself as much as possible for what I knew was coming.

I remember talking to one particularly amazing and helpful woman who loves physical fitness, running, and is incredibly in shape. She answered all of my questions beautifully and gave me great insight on the road that was ahead of me. She shared a bit about her journey, and how she continued to run throughout the course of her treatments. In fact, she said she actually ran from her house to the hospital for the last chemo infusion. Wow! I was completely inspired and thought to myself, "That's going to be me. I'm going to keep working out, and I'm going to show these treatments who's boss!" Yeah, well, that didn't quite happen. My lofty goal of planking, crunching, and lifting my way through treatment, went out the window on day one, and, honestly, it was a little deflating at first.

By no means do I fault the examples of others who are able to do this and who thrive physically during cancer treatment. In fact, I applaud them and am so inspired by them! But this wasn't my path. I had to remind myself that I wasn't them. I was me. This is how my body was choosing to respond, and I had to embrace and respect that. Treatment courses are different for everyone. Sometimes the actual chemo cocktail of drugs is different, or the frequency of the treatment administration is more or less, and sometimes it's just the way our bodies are made and how they respond to the drugs. Whatever the difference is, you have to remind yourself that everyone and every situation is different.

Recovery time is another area that can be easy to compare ourselves to others. For me, it took me around a year after my last treatment to begin to really feel myself and have my energy back. You may talk to people who said they were back to work a week after the last treatment or who actually worked full time through the whole treatment process! Again, I think that's amazing! But that's not everyone's story. It's important to listen to your body. Restrain from the mental gymnastics that our minds can go through when we feel like we are failing in some way because all we want to do is sit on the couch and watch the Hallmark Channel instead of putting in a strong work day. You will get there in time, and this is where that grace thing comes into play again.

It's also easy to compare our appearance to others. When my hair was growing back, I searched Pinterest and Google for pixie hairstyles and often came across a time-lapse video or photo collages of other cancer survivors and their hair growth timelines. I would look at these and think, "Okay. First of all, my hair is nowhere near that cute, nor is it growing back as fast as these women. Seriously? A bob in six months? Whatever! I'll be lucky to get past the Cosmo Kramer from the TV show, *Seinfeld*, stage in a year!"

Everyone recovers differently, and the physical aspect is no different. Some women will have hair that grows back crazy curly, or thicker, or thinner, or darker, or grayer, but ultimately you just don't know what your outcome will be until you experience it. No matter what that outcome is, it's uniquely you. You may lose all of your eyebrows and eyelashes, and someone else may keep every perfect hair on their face. It's all okay.

The same concept goes for our emotional state. You may feel defeated because someone else seems strong as stone and flying through it like a boss, but you are a constant puddle and feel incredibly weak. It's okay. You know when you can feel strong and when you need to allow yourself to be that puddle.

So, remember, it's YOUR journey, and there is no right or wrong. You're not a failure or somehow inadequate when it comes to your path. If you're one of those people who is rocking the workout routine or regrowing perfectly coiffed, thick tresses, then punch cancer in the face on a daily basis and celebrate! But if you're not, that's okay, too! Everyone who experiences a trial like cancer is a rockstar and each is created as an incredible and unique individual.

God made you just the way you are and perfectly crafted you according to His will. Psalm 139:13-14 says, *"For you formed my inward parts; you knitted me together in my mother's womb. I praise you, for I am fearfully and wonderfully made. Wonderful are your works; my soul knows it very well."* You are wonderful and uniquely you, and so is your journey.

34

Don't Let This Define You

Say your name. No seriously, say your name out loud. Right now. That's right. That's who you are. Your name is not cancer. Notice I didn't even give the word, cancer, the satisfaction of capitalizing it. Cancer does not define you, and you shouldn't let it define you even when you feel like it is completely encompassing and overpowering everything about you at the moment. You are still the same person you were before you got the diagnosis and you will be that same person forever. Will your life be changed and will you grow and evolve from that previous person? Absolutely. But it is important to believe that you will not become "cancer." You have the ability to prevent that word from being a burden and label that can weigh you down and steal your identity.

There were a few things I did to help me battle this potential identity theft while I was going through it. I've touched on my love for fashion a bit already, but this is where it really came into play. By no means do I consider myself a fashion expert or the next Victoria Beckham, but I love a great dress and a cute pair of shoes, just like the next girl. I find joy in expressing myself creatively through fashion and have ever since I was a little girl. My mother would be happy to pull out the highly embarrassing pictures of me as a child with the mismatched socks, fluffy tutus, and multiple colored hair bows to help prove this point. I was actually given the title of "Most Fashionable" by my peers during my senior year in high school, and I have my Madonna-inspired neon earrings, oversized jackets with shoulder pads, and stirrup pants to thank for that. So, I made the decision that even though I was battling cancer and not exactly feeling like breaking out my fanciest formal gown, I wasn't going to let cancer steal something that I loved.

I made a conscious effort to get up each morning and get dressed. Yes, some mornings it was sweatpants and a t-shirt, but if I was actually venturing out of the house, I took some time and picked out an outfit that I felt good in. I decided to take pride in my appearance, even though I was bald, my eyes were a little sunken in and dark, and my skin was an absolute disaster. I put on some makeup (a lot of it was needed some days) and always picked a cheery color of lipstick to top it off. It was my way of saying to cancer that it didn't have a hold over me. I shopped for pretty scarves and worked to coordinate them with my outfits and then find creative ways to tie them around my head.

One day I was feeling particularly adventurous with my scarf antics and tied a pretty turban with a fun twisty knot, placed slightly off center of my forehead. I was loving it and having a blast trying out new turban styles. I had an appointment with my oncologist that day for a checkup, and as I was riding in the elevator after the appointment, I noticed a lady standing across from me, eyeing me up and down with a strange look on her face. She opened her mouth and dripping with sarcasm she said, "Well, that's an interesting headdress you have on." Really? Really, lady? Don't you see that I'm leaving the ONCOLOGY department? I replied with a smile, "Why, thank you!" and promptly swished past her as the elevator doors opened. I'll be honest, it did hurt my feelings a little, but I vowed right then and there that I was not going to let a snarky old lady, or a nasty disease, make me feel any less of myself. God made me the way I am for a reason and making a conscious effort to hold on to that gave me some power over this disease. Be determined not to let a disease or a bad situation steal those pieces of you that make you feel like, you.

One of the other crazy things I did after my last treatment to maintain a sense of "me," was have a dear friend, who is a professional photographer, take some photos of me while I was bald. I'm sure you're probably thinking either, "There is no way in H.E. double hockey sticks I would do that!" Or "Geez, that's pretty vain of you!"

I understand where both of those reactions come from. Losing your hair, as a woman, is pretty traumatic and if this has happened to you or is currently happening, I can see where you would want to either forget this moment in your life altogether or at least never have it documented for posterity. However, I had a very strong desire to do just that. I believed in my heart that there would be a time when I would be able to look back on this horrible time in my life and see it as a distant memory. What I was afraid of, is that I would forget. I was afraid of forgetting how it changed me for the better and that, somehow, I would lose all recollection of that dark place that I learned so much from. So, I decided to document it.

I coordinated a date with both the photographer and another friend who is a makeup artist, and we got to work. I made a point to schedule it on a day when I knew I would be feeling relatively well and would have enough energy to make it through without collapsing into a useless mess. The makeup artist came to my home, and she promptly started using her foundation airbrush spray gun.... all over my head. Now, if that isn't an experience you can chalk up to something that you've never done before, I don't know what is! She sprayed away all over my bald scalp and face and then finished with a very natural look on my eyes and cheeks.

We began the photo session, taking some pictures that captured the raw emotion of what I was experiencing, and I allowed my bulging port just below my collarbone to take front and center a few times. Again, I wanted to record this moment and all the realness about it, not only for me but for my daughters.

After we felt that we had successfully gotten those more natural images, we moved onto something a little more fun. I asked the makeup artist to glam me up a bit and to give me some much-needed eyelashes and eyebrows. I wanted to feel beautiful and ignite that little bit of spark inside that I knew was me, but had been taking a beating for some time now. I put on a fun outfit, cranked up a little Beyoncé, and we had a picture-taking party. The result was a super fun compilation of images that encompassed both the somber and the survivor spirit. I remember leaving the downtown building where we shot the pictures, walking across the busy street to my car, bald head exposed for all to see, and feeling absolutely exhausted, but beautiful and alive.

So, find that thing that makes you feel like you, and dig deep inside and pull it out. Let whatever that thing is, shine brighter than the disease like a flashlight in a dark cave. A beam of light can pierce the blackness and fight back the shadows if you simply turn it on. If you're a writer, then write like crazy. If you love to bake or knit, get out those mixing bowls or knitting needles and go to town. If you love earrings, then rock the most fabulous earrings you can find, like nobody's business!

Don't lose yourself in the darkness while fighting your way to the light. Matthew 5:15 says, *"Neither do people light a lamp and put it under a bowl. Instead, they put it on its stand, and it gives light to everyone in the house."* Don't let your situation own you. It's not okay to refer to your disease as "MY cancer." It is not yours. It doesn't own you unless you allow it. And if you stand up to it with who you really are in Christ, it never will.

35

You Can Choose Your Voice

If you're a cancer survivor, you have a choice. You can choose the voice you have regarding your journey and the disease in general. Everyone is different in the way they feel about their experience and in the way they choose to express it. Some are very private and don't want to think about it or talk about it with anyone. That's fine. That's their choice, and I absolutely respect that. Some have the need to talk about it all the time and put stickers of colored awareness ribbons on their car bumpers or even tattoo them on their bodies. That's fine, too! That's their choice, and I absolutely respect that as well. What is important is that you do what feels right for you.

Just because you have experienced cancer doesn't mean you have to become the poster child for the cause of finding a cure or educating others about the disease. It doesn't have to be your banner that you take up and wave relentlessly at every cancer walk or fundraiser. Yes, it is a chapter in the book that is your life and a very big chapter at that, but it doesn't have to be the overall theme of your existence if you don't want it to be.

Now, on the other hand, I have found that having gone through this trial, has given me a heavy, but important responsibility. I have been overwhelmed by the number of women who have reached out to me sharing similar diagnoses and searching for answers to questions, a listening ear, or just someone to help them feel like they aren't alone. I remember being in their shoes when I first found out I had cancer and how I frantically searched for information and answers. But what I desired more than simple answers to medical questions was real experiences, had by real people who had walked this road before me. There is a comfort knowing that someone else can relate to the rollercoaster of feelings and physical ups and downs that you are going through. And when someone is struggling, they are often desperate for any tips or tricks to help them along the way.

So, I encourage you to share your story. If you feel comfortable letting others into your world even a little, it can make a huge difference in their lives. It doesn't have to be much. It can be a phone call or a brief meeting over coffee.

So often I feel like we wrap up our pain and stuff it in the closet so no one can ever see it. But there is someone out there suffering from the same kind of pain you have experienced that could use your encouragement. There is no better way to take something awful and use it for good, than by giving your story to someone else.

When I meet with a newly diagnosed woman for the first time and listen, share my experience, and sometimes cry alongside them, there is something that happens inside of me that feels a little like healing. It takes a lot of time to heal emotionally from a trauma like this, and that healing is multi-faceted. For me, talking about it with others who are struggling is one of those ways that helps heal my soul. It's a way for me to process my pain, grief, and anger so that it doesn't stay bottled up inside festering and growing only to suddenly reemerge sometime when I'm not expecting it.

It also gives me power over the disease knowing that I am taking this horrible thing and using it for good. Genesis 50:20 says, *"You intended to harm me, but God intended it for good to accomplish what is now being done, the saving of many lives."* Don't miss out on the blessing your story can be not only for someone else but also for you.

It's alright to move on with your life after cancer, and I encourage you to do so! But consider being a light to others around you when it's appropriate, and if you're feeling called to that responsibility. Allowing God to use you to be His hands and feet is both incredibly fulfilling and needed. He needs soft hearts and vulnerable spirits that are willing to remove the veil from our own hurts, failures, and struggles so we can come alongside others with love and empathy. The coolest part is that the gift you're giving to others will come right back and be a beautiful and unexpected blessing for yourself.

36

How Do I Pick Up the Pieces?

Once I finished my traditional treatments and surgery and was given permission to move on with my life, I realized that I had just entered a strange new phase of this journey that was very confusing. I had been fighting for what felt like so long and was blessed with friends and family rallying around me every step of the way. Once I was out of the woods, that all changed. Of course, my support team was still there, but it was as if all the cheerleaders at the football game had picked up their pom-poms and had gone home. I was left standing in the end zone celebrating my win, but quickly realizing the stadium was emptying, and I was exhausted and completely beat up from the full-contact battle I had just waged.

People assume that once you're done with the things that they can see like chemo, surgery, or any other type of medical treatments, then you are good to go and are able to jump back into life as though you had never left. However, that is the furthest thing from the truth. A bomb has literally gone off inside your body and in your mind, and you are left picking up the pieces and trying to somehow fit them back together. It's also particularly confusing to people because to them you look great. You're out in public a bit, you have a little color back in your face, and your hair might even be growing in at this point. But I remember still feeling incredibly weak, lacking in my normal energy, and still riding that emotional rollercoaster that was giving me a run for my money.

I found that people expected me to jump into responsibilities or time commitments that I used to take part in before my diagnosis, and I don't fault them for having the assumption that I could just pick up where I left off. But I knew that I was nowhere near ready for those things, and I needed to set boundaries for myself. I had to respect my body and my mind and make sure that I was doing what was best for me and my recovery. If that meant taking regular naps in the middle of the day and saying no to that request from a friend for a lunch date, or volunteer community board meeting, then that is what I had to do. It was hard. I'm not going to lie. All I wanted to do was to run full speed back into the life that was stolen from me, and there were days when I would get very sad and frustrated because I couldn't do just that.

During those times I would grab a cup of tea, go sit on my patio and watch the birds. I started making a list of what I wanted my priorities to be in life. I realized that I had just been given a huge reset button and I could begin my life fresh with new eyes and a new perspective. I could start over and begin putting things first that had been last, and finally purge junk that used to be pesky time suckers.

I prioritized the list according to how I wanted to spend my time. I listed the things that were most important to me such as my relationship with God, my family, friends, writing, community involvement, etc. Then, I also wrote down the things that were keeping me from those priorities. For example, social media scrolling and organizations that I had been volunteering with that I didn't have a true passion for.

I began cutting out those extraneous things and building in time not only for what I was passionate about, but also times for me to rest. That part was HARD. But I kept reflecting on those past moments when I was forced to be still during my treatments and how God spoke to me so beautifully during those quiet times. I made a vow to myself that I would not allow the busyness of my world, rob me of those peaceful instances that not only refreshed my soul, but also my body. Unfortunately, this is a constant battle and one that I have to continue to wage war against, but at least being aware of it, is half the fight.

I also had to begin picking up the pieces of my emotional well-being. I can't begin to imagine what our nation's brave servicemen and women go through when they experience the trauma of war. I know that, unfortunately, many suffer from post-traumatic stress disorder. My experience doesn't even compare to what many of them have dealt with and maybe still do, but I feel that there is a level of PTSD that a cancer survivor goes through when they come out from the other side.

I still had a lot of physical pain that I was dealing with from my mastectomy and also the weakness in my muscles due to the chemotherapy. My quadriceps actually burned when I walked, and it wasn't because I had worked out hard. No, it was because of how weak and strained they were from inactivity and the chemotherapy drugs. I would also have flashbacks months down the road when my hair started growing back, but would naturally shed into my brush. My heart would begin to pound, and I would immediately go back to those days in the shower when clumps were coming out in my hands. Those memories would flood back in extreme detail and I would be transported to that horrible place in my mind.

I also experienced incredible grief. I mourned the person I was before the diagnosis and even looking at pictures of myself was painful. I saw innocence and youthfulness in the face looking back at me from those images, and I missed that person. I missed the physical things like my hair and eyelashes and often thought about what it would be like to travel back in time and tell that happy-go-lucky girl with the ponytail top knot on her head to enjoy that hairstyle while she can and not complain about the zit on her forehead. Even two years later, I still mourn that girl on occasion.

There were times that I found myself withdrawing and avoiding people simply because I was tired of everyone asking, "How are you feeling?" Crappy. I feel crappy, darn it. Of course, I was thankful for the concern that people showed toward my situation, but many times I simply wanted to forget. Is there a better question for people to ask? I don't know, but this was my reality, and I had to take the focus off of myself and my feelings and understand that they were simply trying to show their care and concern. And I truly did appreciate the concern.

However, the takeaway that I learned from being on the other side of an illness, is the importance of approaching those, who are having health challenges, with compassion coupled with a cheery and positive attitude. The big smiles, the "You look great!", comments or even a compliment about my shoes helped keep the focus off of the struggle and kept me feeling more upbeat when interacting with others.

Emotional recovery is still a challenging mental game, and as time went on, I realized that there was really no good way to describe what was spinning around in my head. There was a part of me that wanted to pretend that cancer never even happened, so the constant reminders were tough some days. These were things that I struggled with as I emerged from those dark months, and I knew that I needed help to get through it.

It's important to seek that help, and there are many great resources out there that are available to tap into. Trained professionals, like therapists, are great for talking through your feelings and processing the trauma. Oftentimes, they can reveal different perspectives and give you tools to help you work through those difficult moments. There have been times in my life when I have experienced incredible healing from working with a therapist, and I am grateful for their expertise. However, in this situation my therapist was Jesus.

During those quiet moments that I had purposefully scheduled in my day, I would cry out to God with my hurts and struggles. I asked Him for help to show me how to navigate through these unfamiliar waters of recovery and to give me wisdom. I learned to speak life and truth over myself and would say Bible verses out loud when I was feeling particularly weak or withdrawn. One of my favorites was Romans 8:36-39 which says, *"As it is written: "For your sake we face death all day long; we are considered as sheep to be slaughtered." No, in all these things we are more than conquerors through him who loved us. For I am convinced that neither death nor life, neither angels nor demons, neither the present nor the future, nor any powers, neither height nor depth, nor anything else in all creation, will be able to separate us from the love of God that is in Christ*

Jesus our Lord." This verse gave me strength, knowing that no matter what happened or how I was feeling that day, I was a conqueror because God loves me and nothing, not even cancer, would be able to separate me from His love.

Romans 8:28 was another one I used when I felt like I had lost myself and was never going to see anything good come from what I had just faced. *"And we know in that all things God works for the good of those who love him, who have been called according to his purpose."* The word I had to focus on a lot was the word, ALL. It doesn't say that a few things work together for good, no, it says ALL things work together for good for them that love God. Even though I didn't understand it then, I began telling myself that God can take this pain and make something good come out of it.

Once I started speaking these truths over me and believing them in my heart, I started to feel the fog lift a little, and the pieces begin to slowly fit back together one by one. It's interesting though. Unlike the Christmas puzzle that I unpack from the basement for my family every year and spread out on a card table during the holiday season; the pieces I was putting back together weren't creating the same picture they had once before. The picture they were creating looked considerably different. God was rearranging my life and giving me a new vision and purpose that would never have emerged had it not been for the trial. That new picture that He will create in your life if you let Him, is beautiful. Different, yes. But beautiful, nonetheless. The pieces will slowly fit back together in a seamless fashion, and the visible cracks between the pieces will be reminders of the brokenness we had to go through. But the image that will eventually be created will far surpass and outshine those cracks that made the realization of that outcome possible.

37

In Sickness and In Health...

Life can be extremely stressful, and life stresses can take a significant toll on your marriage. I've often been given the advice to try to avoid experiencing more than one life-changing event within a year's period of time to help safeguard against a crushing strain on my relationship with my husband. For example, having a baby, moving to a new house or city, and starting a new job all within a twelve-month period can be a tad stressful on a marriage. Obviously, situations like this can't always be avoided, but when presented with a choice, it's better to spread out major life changes or decisions to avoid getting your world completely rocked off the rails.

Going through something like cancer is like doing all of the above on steroids. When we took our marriage vows and promised that we would love each other through "sickness and in health," in my ideal little world, I always imaged those words simply referring to those days when one of us was stricken with a nasty flu bug. In my mind, it consisted of one bringing the other some chicken noodle soup and running to the store for some more Tylenol when needed. But facing a life-threatening disease just wasn't on my radar when I gazed into my husband's handsome, and nervously excited face, on our wedding day.

"Sickness and in health" meant way, way down the road when we were old and grey, swaying back and forth in our rocking chairs, watching the sunset of our lives slowly set, naturally and organically. Hold the phone, people! This was not my idea of "sickness and in health!" I never in a million years thought that only nine and a half years into our marriage we would be faced with a life-altering health crisis. A crisis of this magnitude can be incredibly stressful on a relationship, and Andrew and I were definitely not immune to those stresses.

When a woman is diagnosed with breast cancer, so much of the focus is on her and rightfully so, but the partner often gets left out of that support system. I found that there were many resources for me that came in multiple forms such as books, support groups, and websites, but for my husband, the love didn't get shared quite as much. The reality of it was that he was going through this just as much as I was, and there were real struggles and emotions that he was feeling that needed to be acknowledged and processed. We were both worried about how this was going to affect our marriage, and we decided to make the conscious choice to be intentional in finding ways to combat the assault we knew we were in for as a couple.

One of Andrew's fears, in the beginning, was how he was going to take care of me, our daughters, our home, and run his family's business. Up until this point, we had created a fairly well-oiled machine between the two of us, in terms of family and work-life balance. We each had our specific responsibilities, both at home and at work, that kept our lives ticking along each day, and when one person lacked, the other would fill in. But in an instant, one half of that machine had broken down, and the other half had to keep the whole contraption in motion all by himself. That is a huge responsibility, and the pressure of that weighed very heavily on Andrew. Even with the wonderful help that we received from our friends and family, there were still a lot of gaps that he had to fill.

We remember starting the fight those early weeks, after the diagnosis, with a fairly high level of energy and strength, but as time went on and the days turned into weeks which turned into months, we became weary. I could see the strain it was putting on him. One particular day, close to dinner time, we were in the kitchen, and we didn't have a plan for dinner. Couple that with being new to the plant-based diet we had recently adopted, and we were scrambling to figure out something for us and the girls to eat. I wasn't much help, and I could see the pressure of this seemingly simple task beginning to build in Andrew. After searching through the refrigerator and the pantry for something he could put together, and coming up empty, he leaned on the kitchen counter and hung his head. I noticed his shoulders begin to shake and the tears started to flow. The weight of what he had been carrying for so long had finally broken him. He had been so strong for me for all those past months, but the reality was he was tired, and, rightfully so. He had been so faithful, caring, and patient, but he was also human, and there's only so much that one person can take.

I walked up to him, put my arms around his waist, and told him that everything was going to be okay. I could see that he was completely overwhelmed, and I reassured him that we would find something easy to eat, and that take-out was only a phone call away. I told him that it was okay to take the pressure off of himself to be everything to everyone, including me. As much as seeing him break like this again after so long, shocked me at first, I was thankful that it happened. It opened up an opportunity for him to be vulnerable again and for us to share with each other how weary we really were. He shared more of his feelings, how he had finally hit a wall, and how the emotional fatigue had set in.

Having this conversation allowed him to validate his emotions and helped dispel any initial thoughts of failure on his part. I believe our partners need to be reassured that it's normal to feel completely overwhelmed and ill-equipped at times to be our caregivers on top of all of the other responsibilities they have. This is a very normal feeling, especially for those husbands who are "fixers" and tend to put pressure on themselves to be able to manage everything at all times. This breakthrough was so helpful and needed as we neared the last part of this journey, which is often the most difficult due to the sheer length of the trial. So, after we pulled ourselves together, reassured each other that it was fine to let things go, and admit that we were tired, we dialed the neighborhood Vietnamese restaurant and ordered a boatload of vegetarian egg rolls.

We have found, that as a couple, trials can either squeeze you together or push you apart. A house divided against itself cannot stand so I can't stress enough the importance of trying to maintain a united front. We made a conscious choice to not allow this difficulty to be that wedge that can so easily divide two people who love each other. You're probably thinking, "Oh sure, so easily said than done!" You're absolutely right. It's not easy, and we were by no means experts and definitely struggled with this at times.

But the one thing we did do that helped tremendously, was to communicate with each other as much as humanly possible. We also went into it knowing that incredible stress can divide two people so having that knowledge right off the bat was like being on a sports team and reading the opponent's playbook before a game. We already knew what to expect, so when the stress and strain began, we could see it for what it was, and acknowledge it. If you aren't intentional about recognizing it early, that wedge can slowly begin to tap itself into place right between the two of you without you even realizing it. If you stay in front of it, that potential wedge will be much easier to manage and, hopefully, avoid altogether. The way we did that was through a LOT of talking.

Ladies, you may be thinking, "Hallelujah!" Preach that sister! In general, we women connect and feel love when we are able to express ourselves through words. However, verbal communication doesn't always come as easy to our male counterparts, but it's so important to work through that and try to share your thoughts and feelings with each other as much as possible.

You have to be real with where you're at physically, and emotionally and also share what you need from the other person. For us, this was a wide spectrum. In terms of my needs, it was everything from telling him that I needed a piece of toast with almond butter, pronto, because I was feeling lightheaded, (and of course asking nicely if he wouldn't mind fixing it for me) to how I just needed him to simply hug me when I was upset and crying with no expectation of him trying to fix how I was feeling.

For Andrew, it was him telling me he needed to get away with his guy friends and go for a really long bike ride to de-stress. He also needed to have opportunities to discuss his life outside of my battle with cancer which included his work and his responsibilities there. Before my diagnosis, this was something we shared frequently with each other, and he needed that communication about his professional life to remain the same. So, sharing that these conversations were still important to him, was helpful for me to know that I needed to set aside time to focus on him.

One other thing that was very helpful was discussing and agreeing that anytime one of us needed to talk or express an issue we had with the other, that those concerns would be met with a calm listening ear. One of the things I love about Andrew is that he gives me a safe place to express my thoughts or concerns. He doesn't jump down my throat with excuses or defensive retorts but listens and hears me out.

This is an area that I realized I needed to work on, and his example was helpful for me to recognize that. I have a tendency to get defensive and justify my actions when someone puts the mirror up for me, but I learned quickly that this isn't helpful. Being defensive only makes the other person shut down and not feel free to truly express what is on their heart. Creating that safe place to be vulnerable and honest opens up better opportunities for deeper communication that will help you and your partner better navigate this crazy life and all of the fireballs that get thrown at you. So, talk, talk, talk, and when you feel like you're done talking, be ready to talk some more. Communication is the ultimate relationship "wedge buster"!

Being squeezed during this season of our life made us stronger. Our communication improved, and it helped us become more comfortable being real and transparent about what we each needed. Now it's much more natural for us to share when we need help with something, whether it's a chore around the house, a night with girlfriends to fill up my social bucket, or an extra-long workout for him to de-stress. It even helped us learn how to communicate better with our children. Again, this takes being intentional and having both parties in agreement that strength and unity is the end goal. So, put on those matching jerseys and start playing on the same team. You're both in this together!

38

The Elephant in the Room

I am literally squirming and nervously sucking down my venti, decaf, hot, Americano like a crazy person right now because I know I have to address what no one wants to talk about, but everyone wants to hear. It's the big, fat elephant in the room that, surprisingly, I get asked about all the time by women who are going through a similar diagnosis as I did. It's physical intimacy. Oh yes, I am going to go there. Not because I want to, but because it's a real issue that couples struggle with when the wife has been diagnosed with cancer and is facing chemotherapy treatments that can potentially have a huge effect on this important area of a relationship.

During those initial days when we were hit with the devastating news that I had cancer, we were given so much information about what to expect, potential side effects from chemotherapy, and more. Being the researcher that he is, Andrew dove into these materials and read most of them cover to cover. Big mistake. Yes, it can be helpful to familiarize yourself with the process, and it's good to be educated, but for Andrew, it sent him into a tailspin of worry and despair. In his mind, these particular materials painted a very bleak picture of our future in terms of physical intimacy.

Chemotherapy has the potential to put women into early menopause and with that, comes symptoms such as fatigue, night sweats, hot flashes, insomnia, the absence of menstrual cycles or irregular menstrual cycles, irritability, moodiness, vaginal dryness, and reduced sex drive. Well, as you can imagine, Andrew was very concerned about the possibility of me experiencing these symptoms in my very near future and, honestly, it freaked him out. As a woman, menopause is always something that you know you're going to experience at some point in your life, naturally, but you are never really prepared for the thought of it happening almost instantly, especially when you think you have a little time left. For us, the same was true for Andrew, and he was very concerned about what our future would look like in this area.

Having a healthy physical relationship is important to any marriage, and we both knew that. Andrew struggled quite a bit with feeling selfish for worrying that this part of our marriage was going to suffer or worse yet, be completely non-existent. Typically, men find a connection with their partner through physical intimacy, and when that is strong, they are more apt to open up emotionally. Women tend to be the opposite and feel freer and safer to be engaged physically when they can connect emotionally first. Andrew was concerned that if one area was lacking that it would create a dangerous cycle that might affect our closeness as a couple. But again, he felt incredibly guilty because I was fighting for my life, and he was concerned about his sexual needs. But it was real, and something he was really wrestling with.

He knew he needed to work through these anxious feelings of fear, and he began crying out to God for help. God gently showed Andrew that once again he was fighting Him and His sovereignty. Andrew felt the Lord say, "Hey, do you trust Me, and do you trust that I have your wife?" This was the breakthrough that Andrew needed, and He prayed that God would lessen his desire during this season, help him to trust Him more, and also that God would teach him how to serve me better. It wasn't until he made this conscious decision to trust God with our intimacy that he was finally able to let it go. He also prayed that God would help him to continue to find me physically attractive even as I lost my hair and became a physical shell of what I once was. Andrew desperately wanted to still find me beautiful, and that was exactly what happened when he surrendered his anxiety to the Lord.

The other thing that helped change Andrew's mindset from one of despair to hope was talking with other husbands whose wives also went through premature menopause due to chemo. Those men were instrumental in reassuring him that there is life after treatment and that it's not all doom and gloom. They explained that their physical intimacy didn't disappear, but it just changed. They went on to stress the importance of being more creative and intentional with finding ways to get around those things that can put a damper on intimacy whether they were physical, like vaginal dryness, or emotional, like lack of desire.

There was a big part that I had to play in all of this, too, and that was validating his feelings and keeping the communication lines open. You absolutely have to talk about this with each other, and don't spare any details! It may feel strange to be so vulnerable with what's going through your head when it comes to physical intimacy, but I can tell you that the only way you can move forward, let alone through an issue like this, is by being very transparent.

Andrew will be the first to tell me that he is "clueless" when it comes to knowing what I'm thinking and what is going through my head. Ladies, news flash! Men can't read our minds! They need to know exactly what you want and need, and that can only happen when you TELL them. I found that letting Andrew speak freely about his thoughts and fears in this area was crucial, but I also shared what I needed. One of my big requests was simply patience. I knew things would get better, but it was going to take time. I also told him that I needed him to tell me I was beautiful. Insecurity can easily creep in when you look in the mirror and see Mr. Clean looking back at you. Trust me. It's a real confidence buster in the bedroom department, so any time Andrew verbally validated that he still found me attractive was huge for me. It made me feel safe, and when I feel safe, I'm more likely to open up and be more comfortable with intimacy.

Another thing that helped us tremendously was what we like to call,

"If not now, then when?" If I wasn't feeling well enough to be physically intimate, or just not feeling it in general, I would tell him. But instead of completely shutting him down and making him feel hopelessly rejected, I instead told him when a better time would be. This simple practice helped ease his mind and took away any worry he might have had, otherwise, that may have kept him wondering for days, weeks, or worse!

There are other practical ways to keep that flame alive. One of my favorite things we did as a couple, and I also think one of the most healing, was getting away for a weekend after I was physically in the clear. I had finished all of my chemo treatments and had relatively healed from my surgery, so we booked a weekend at a spa an hour or so away from our home. We left the kids with my parents and spent the entire weekend cocooned in glorious isolation. We used the time to reflect on what we had just been through, talked about what we want our next season to look like, and then spent time praying together. We prayed specifically for our physical intimacy, but also for our relationship, in general, moving forward. We asked God to continue to protect our marriage and to bless it by making it stronger. I remember leaving that spa after those couple of wonderful days feeling renewed and reset as a couple.

Dating is key. You need to date your spouse on a regular basis! Even if you're in the thick of your fight, set time to have a date. If you're not feeling like leaving the house, then order takeout from your favorite restaurant, send the kids to a friend's home for the evening, and light a couple of candles. Even an hour or two of talking and connecting will help with intimacy on all levels.

If you find yourself in the same boat we were, and physical intimacy is a concern for you or your husband, I want to tell you this. Don't freak out! It's not a hopeless situation, and there is a light at the end of the tunnel. It may not look like it was before, and those chandeliers you were swinging on as newlyweds might get a little dusty, but there is hope and a future for you both if you release your concerns to God and be intentional about your approach to your relationship. God can make all things new so trust that the changes and differences you are experiencing in your physical relationship are simply reconfigurations. Instead of having a mindset that the sexual intimacy you used to have is gone, think of it as a new beginning and simply a different, yet still wonderful, version of what it once was. So, there you have it. I did it. Consider the "elephant" officially addressed, and now I'm going to crawl under the couch.

39

Where is My Hope?

We all have the capacity to hope for something, and I'm sure you can name many things you have hoped for in the past. I know I have hoped that the superfly coat I've been coveting on the Nordstrom's website will go on sale at some point for starters. Maybe you have hope that your favorite football team who has stunk all season will still pull off a minor miracle and make it to the playoffs. My daughters have hope that someday we will get a dog, and they remind us on a daily basis how they will take care of it, walk it, and pick up poop all while never being asked to do so. Ever. (Oh sure.) But no matter what the scenario, the thing that keeps us going and not giving up on whatever it is that we have our heart set on, is the hope of a positive outcome.

Some days it's hard to have hope, especially if you're struggling with a major health concern or life issue. In my case, my hope was that I would someday be free of cancer and never have to go through this experience again. I am incredibly grateful that I am a survivor, and have had a clean bill of health for over two years, and counting. My hope is that I will live a long and fruitful life and be gently taken from this world in my old age, after watching my children have children. But I also know that this may not be my path. I could be taken home to Heaven tomorrow by a speeding Schwan's truck! Even though I believe in my heart, and have confidence that I am healed, I also know that God's plan for me is just that. His plan. I continue to release my health into His hands daily and trust that no matter what happens, I am His.

I understand that there may be someone reading this right now that doesn't have a favorable health prognosis, and for that, I am truly sorry that this is something you are dealing with. But I want to tell you that there is still hope. You can still have hope, knowing that there is a God who loves you and desires to have a relationship with you. There is a Heavenly Father who cares for you as a cherished son or daughter and desires to pour out His goodness and blessing on you even through the most difficult times in your life. Romans 8:22-25 says, *"We know that the whole creation has been groaning as in the pains of childbirth right up to the present time. Not only so, but we ourselves, who have the firstfruits of the Spirit, groan inwardly as we wait eagerly for our adoption as sons, and the redemption of our bodies. For in this hope we were saved. But hope that is seen is no hope at all. Who hopes for what he already has? But if we hope for what we do not yet have, we wait for it patiently."*

If you have put your faith in Jesus Christ, you have a hope and a future, no matter what the outcome is here on this earth. You have a Father who will never break His promises to you, and one of those many promises is that God is FOR us! We are more than conquerors because God sent His Son, Jesus, to die for us so that we may live in eternity in the glorious presence of our Creator. Romans 8:31-32 *"...If God is for us, who can be against us? He who did not spare his own Son, but gave him up for us all—how will he not also, along with him, graciously give us all things?"* When you believe in Jesus, nothing can separate you from His love, even death.

The best part about all of this is that it's easy! You can have this glorious hope every day of your life no matter what you are dealing with. It's not a secret concoction, magic formula, or endless to-do list of works you have to accomplish. Nope, it's simply believing in your heart that Jesus is the Son of God and that He died and rose to life again to forgive us of our sins. It's confessing with your mouth that Jesus is Lord and telling God that you need Him and want Him in your life. It's truly that simple.

Does this guarantee that your life will be trouble-free? Of course not. But it does guarantee that you will have hope, both in this life and the next. It gives you the peace to know that no matter what happens, you will spend an eternity with the Father in heaven. This is my hope. This is what keeps me going every day, and what helps me keep my earthly troubles in perspective. Yes, it is hard. Yes, there is pain. But I have HOPE, and I know that my God loves me and will see me through. No matter what.

40

I Have Two Words For You

This journey has been an experience that some days seems like a distant memory, and yet it's always at the forefront of my mind. It's changed me, but I believe for the better. I have lost so much, and yet I've gained so much more. I have captured a deeper appreciation of the inner strength I never thought I had and an even greater appreciation of my many weaknesses. I have lived in the depths of desperation, and experienced the saving grace and faithfulness of God, and have walked through the fire.

This couldn't be better illustrated than in one of my favorite stories in the Book of Daniel. It is about three guys in dire need of some good nicknames who also experienced surviving the fire in a very literal sense. Shadrach, Meshach, and Abednego were friends who were thrown into a fiery furnace because they refused the order given by King Nebuchadnezzar to bow down to a golden statue. Consequently, they were bound and subjected to certain death because of their faithfulness to God and their resolve to not worship any other gods. To everyone's surprise, especially the king's, a fourth person was seen walking around with them in the fire, and this person looked *"like the son of the gods."* All three men walked out of the furnace, unbounded, and completely unharmed.

What struck me about this story was not just the miracle that they were completely spared without even one hair singed, but that God was with them in the furnace. He could have simply waved His hand from the heavens and put the fire out allowing them to walk free, but no. He chose to be in the fire with them, standing beside them, while the flames leaped all around their bodies. He didn't leave them alone in the furnace but instead was right there the whole time. Shadrach, Meshach, and Abednego trusted that their God had the ability to save them. They also acknowledged that if He chose not to, that they would still never serve another god or worship images of gold. This incredible level of trust is hard to comprehend, but it's exactly what they needed to endure the trial they were facing.

The "fires" of life will come and, yes, they are difficult to endure. But allowing them to refine us and gently bubble up the imperfections and areas of our lives that need a closer look, is one of the beautiful outcomes if we put our trust in God. These same difficulties are also opportunities to experience the incredible love of our Savior and grow our relationship with Him in ways we could never imagine. He will shower you with love and deepen the bond that He longs to have with you. His mighty abilities will have a chance to shine in your life and become center stage above all things. The power that was shown in the story about the fiery furnace is the same power that is available to you when you believe and put your trust in Him. I personally had to learn, through my battle with breast cancer, the true meaning of trust and what that looked like in my life.

I needed to trust in the doctors that they had my health and best interest at heart as they used their knowledge to develop and execute a plan. I had to trust in the incredible friends and family that surrounded me with their support through meals, caring for my children, or simply praying for me. But most importantly, I had to trust in God. He alone holds us in the palm of His hand and will never let us go. Trusting is believing in His promises no matter what the circumstances and one of his promises is "perfect peace." Isaiah 26:3 says, *"You will keep in perfect peace those whose minds are steadfast because they trust in you."* You can trust that He loves you and that your health or situation is in His hands. You can trust that His perfect will is at work in your life even if you can't see it right now. You can trust that no matter how hard the trials that you face become, He will see you through to the other side.

Trust will be the most important weapon in your arsenal as you fight this battle. Especially in those times when that trust only feels like a whisper, and you are surrounded by what feels like complete darkness. When we are in darkness, we can better see the light. Those bleak and murky moments are the times when His radiance will shine brighter and be a saving beacon in the storm. He is the same yesterday, today, and forever.

As I reflect back to that little girl He cared for so many years ago, crying over the pain of a sandbur, I can see how He was gently building my trust in Him so that when the true trials came, I would be able to put my hand in His with childlike faith and believe that He would never leave me. The same promise is true for you. *"Blessed is she who has believed that the Lord would fulfill his promises to her!" Luke 1:45.* Write this verse down and stick it on your mirror, or on the dash of your car as a daily reminder that you are not alone and that there is hope.

I have had the privilege of participating in many conversations with women who are facing a similar diagnosis, and I love being able to share my story and encourage them. I am always the first to admit that I don't have all of the answers. However, I know what I experienced and what I lived through. My story is real, and God was there for me in a very real way. He will do that for you, too.

My prayer is that my experience will encourage you and give you hope. I want to tell you that you are going to be okay. So many times, we just need someone to say that. When we are experiencing pain, we desperately want to know that someone else understands what we are going through and that they see us. Living through difficult situations like this can often make you feel invisible. It's easy to ask the question, "Does anyone really see what I'm going through?" I want to tell you that I see you, and I know that God sees me. He knows me and knows what I need, and where I am. He sees you, too. He sees every tear you have shed, and He knows exactly where you are and what you need in this very moment.

You, too, can have hope, and if I could sit down with you, face to face over that cup of coffee, that is exactly what I would say. You may be thinking, "You don't know my situation. It's really bad. I don't know how I'm ever going to get through this." You're right, I don't know your situation, but I know a God who does, who will be there for you every step of the way, and who loves you unconditionally. Give yourself permission to take your hands off of the wheel and rest in the peace of your Creator. Close your eyes and soak in the unconditional love from a Heavenly Father who delights in you just as you are, release your cares and your life to Him, and simply allow yourself to...

TRUST HIM.

Psalm 116
I love the Lord, for he heard my voice;
he heard my cry for mercy.
Because he turned his ear to me,
I will call on him as long as I live.
The cords of death entangled me,
the anguish of the grave came over me;
I was overcome by distress and sorrow.
Then I called on the name of the Lord:
"Lord, save me!"
The Lord is gracious and righteous;
our God is full of compassion.
The Lord protects the unwary;
when I was brought low, he saved me.
Return to your rest, my soul,
for the Lord has been good to you.
For you, Lord, have delivered me from death,
my eyes from tears,
my feet from stumbling,
that I may walk before the Lord
in the land of the living.
I trusted in the Lord when I said,
"I am greatly afflicted";
in my alarm I said,
"Everyone is a liar."
What shall I return to the Lord
for all his goodness to me?
I will lift up the cup of salvation
and call on the name of the Lord.
I will fulfill my vows to the Lord
in the presence of all his people.
Precious in the sight of the Lord
is the death of his faithful servants.

I Have Two Words For You

Truly I am your servant, Lord;
I serve you just as my mother did;
you have freed me from my chains.
I will sacrifice a thank offering to you
and call on the name of the Lord.
I will fulfill my vows to the Lord
in the presence of all his people,
in the courts of the house of the Lord—
in your midst, Jerusalem.

Praise the Lord.

Acknowledgements

First and foremost, I have to thank my incredible husband, Andrew. Your strength carried me through the most difficult season of my life. I am so grateful for your constant love and support. Thank you for believing in me when I struggled to believe in myself. You free me to fly, and I will love you, always.

My daughters, Lauren and Katherine. I am constantly amazed by your strength, resiliency, and your compassion. Even as you walked this difficult time alongside me, you persevered. God blessed me with putting you in my care, and yet during this trial, you cared for me. Thank you for cheering me on, and your nighttime prayers for "Mama's book". God has a plan and purpose for your lives. Never forget that you are daughters of a King. I love you "most-est", to the moon and back, and infinity times 100.

To my parents, Steve and Sandy Brubaker, thank you for always being there through both the triumphs and the tears. You have been my biggest fans, and I am forever grateful. The example that you set is truly inspiring. Thank you for giving me the courage to share my story. I love you both, so much.

My wonderful "Dahl Family", Harry and Carla, Jansen and Kim, and Tyler and Michelle. Thank you for your love, support, caring for our children, and your prayers. Your encouragement has helped me to see this book become a reality. You are all a part of my story, and I am so blessed to have you in my life.

Thank you, Conkwright family, for your inspirational calls and notes, and just being my "fam". You have prayed me through thick and thin. I love you all.

I will forever be thankful for the fantastic physicians and staff at Gundersen Health System for their impeccable care. Thank you, Dr. Leah Dietrich and Eileen Williams PA-C, for your medical expertise and knowledge. Your willingness to "check my work" for medical accuracy, and add your insight to this book, means so much to me.

My sweet friend, Kelly Fernandes. Thank you for walking alongside me from the beginning of this writing journey. Your encouragement, wisdom, and time spent reading through early drafts has been a blessing. Look how far we've come from that kayak ride all those years ago. I love you!

To Suzi Lantz. Thank you for your sensitive spirit, invaluable feedback, and for helping me process through the challenges of writing my first book. I am forever grateful for your encouragement and your insight.

Staci and Larry Wallace, my writing coaches and publisher at EMpowerYOU Publishing. Our friendship is another example of God's beautiful tapestry of life. He wove you both into my world over 20 years ago knowing how instrumental you would be to this project. I am grateful for your editing, graphics, and marketing teams for their care and expertise. Thank you for your wisdom, and for loving me through this process. I am officially your third child, whether you like it or not!

I "do life" better because of these people, Heather and Carl Happel, Charmaine and Tom Kapanke, Dan and Jenn Speckeen, and Anne and Todd Young. Thank you, Life Group, for your encouragement, laughs, and most importantly, your prayers. You all have been a rock for our family.

Paula Koss, my forever friend, thank you for all of the laughter and tears we have shared. You are constant in my life, and I love you.

For my friend who lived this trial alongside me. No one ever chooses to face something like this, but I will forever be grateful for the shared tears, laughs, and very slow walks around the block. We went from coasting down the hills in your stick shift car many years ago without a care in the world to this, but "We lived!" I love you.

My Beautycounter family. The support from all of you is truly inspiring. Thank you for your passion, your heart, and for caring about people well.

To all of my extended family and friends. The way you loved me, served our family, and prayed for me through this difficult season, has blessed me beyond words. To name you all would be book in itself, but you know who you are. I love you all, dearly. You are my people.

Lastly, my Lord and Savior, Jesus Christ. You never leave my side. Thank you, for your not so gentle nudging to write this book. To YOU be the glory!

About the Author

Jamie Dahl has enjoyed a diverse background of life experiences in many areas. She has danced professionally, worked in the fashion industry, taught elementary school, and also worked as an account manager in a marketing company. These professions have taken her all over the country from New York City to Los Angeles, California; Nashville, Tennessee, and Austin, Texas. Her most rewarding job thus far is being a wife and a mom. She now lives in Wisconsin with her husband and two daughters. She also enjoys her current work as a Beautycounter consultant and sharing her faith in God through her powerful story.

Follow Jamie on her blog: **TheDahliaDiaries.com**

Made in the USA
Las Vegas, NV
20 May 2021